Malawi:

Malaria Operational Plan FY 2014

TABLE OF CONTENTS

ABBREVIATIONS AND ACRONYMS

ACT	Artemisinin-based combination therapy
AL	Artemether-lumefantrine
ANC	Antenatal care
ASAQ	Artesunate-amodiaquine
BCC	Behavior change communication
BEST	Best practices at scale in the home, community, and facilities
CBO	Community-based organizations
CCM	Community case management
CDC	Centers for Disease Control and Prevention
CHAI	Clinton Health Access Initiative
CHAM	Christian Health Association of Malawi
CMS	Central Medical Stores Trust
DDT	Dichlorodiphenyltrichloroethane
DfiD	United Kingdom Department for International Development
DHS	Demographic and Health Survey
DHIS	District Health Information System
DHIS 2	District Health Information System Two
DOT	Directly observed therapy
EHP	Essential health package
EMR	Electronic medical record
EPI	Expanded Program on Immunization
EUV	End-use verification
FSN	Foreign service national
FY	Fiscal year
G2G	Government-to-government
GHI	Global Health Initiative
Global Fund	Global Fund to Fight AIDS, Tuberculosis and Malaria
GoM	Government of Malawi
HIV/AIDS	Human immunodeficiency virus/acquired immune deficiency syndrome
HMIS	Health management information system
HRH	Human resources for health
HSA	Health surveillance assistant
HSSP	Health Sector Strategic Plan
HTSS	Health Technical Support Services
IDSR	Integrated Disease Surveillance and Response
IPTp	Intermittent preventive treatment in pregnancy
IRS	Indoor residual spraying
ITN	Insecticide-treated net
IVM	Integrated vector management
ITN	Long-lasting insecticide-treated net
LMIS	Logistics management information system
M&E	Monitoring and evaluation
MAC	Malaria Alert Centre

MALOCAD	Malawi Local Capacity Development
MIP	malaria in pregnancy
MICS	Multiple Indicator Cluster Survey
MIS	Malaria Indicator Survey
MMV	Medicines for Malaria Venture
MOP	Malaria Operational Plan
MoH	Ministry of Health
NGO	Non-governmental organization
NMCP	Malawi National Malaria Control Program
OTSS	Outreach training and support supervision
PBI	Performance Based Incentives
PEPFAR	U.S. President's Emergency Plan for AIDS Relief
PFM	Public Financial Management
PMI	President's Malaria Initiative
QA/QC	Quality assurance/quality control
RBM	Roll Back Malaria
RDT	Rapid diagnostic test
RHU	Reproductive Health Unit
SP	Sulfadoxine-pyrimethamine
SSDI	Support for Service Delivery Integration
SWAp	Sector-wide approach
TDY	Temporary duty
UNICEF	United Nations Children's Fund
USAID	U.S. Agency for International Development
USG	United States Government
VHC	Village health clinic
WHO	World Health Organization

EXECUTIVE SUMMARY

Malaria prevention and control are major foreign assistance objectives of the U.S. Government (USG). In May 2009, President Barack Obama announced the Global Health Initiative (GHI), a six-year, comprehensive effort to reduce the burden of disease and promote healthy communities and families around the world, with a focus on women and girls. The President's Malaria Initiative (PMI) is a core component of the GHI, along with HIV/AIDS and tuberculosis. PMI was launched in June 2005 as a five-year, $1.2 billion initiative to rapidly scale up malaria prevention and treatment interventions and reduce malaria-related mortality by 50% in 15 high-burden countries in sub-Saharan Africa. With passage of the 2008 Lantos-Hyde Act, funding for PMI has now been extended and, as part of the GHI, the goal of PMI has been adjusted to reduce malaria-related mortality by 70% in the original 15 countries by the end of 2015. This will be achieved by continuing to scale up coverage of the most vulnerable groups — children under five years of age and pregnant women — with proven preventive and therapeutic interventions, including artemisinin-based combination therapies (ACTs), insecticide-treated nets (ITNs), intermittent preventive treatment of pregnant women (IPTp), and indoor residual spraying (IRS).

Malawi became a PMI focus country in 2006. It was one of eight countries selected in FY 2011 as a "GHI Plus" country, and receives additional technical and management assistance to rapidly implement GHI's approach. The Ministry of Health's (MoH) National Malaria Control Program (NMCP), with support from PMI and other partners, has been able to scale up the distribution of ACTs, IPTp using sulfadoxine-pyrimethamine (SP), and insecticide-treated nets (ITN), despite a weak health infrastructure. The 2012 Malaria Indicator Survey (MIS) found that 54% of pregnant women reported taking two or more doses of SP for IPTp, which is higher than in many African countries. Additionally, household ITN ownership has increased from 38% in 2006 (Multiple Indicator Cluster Survey, MICS) to 55% in 2012. Similarly, children under five and pregnant women who reported sleeping under an ITN the night prior increased from 25% and 8% in 2006, respectively, to 56% and 51% in 2012.

The 2010 and 2012 MIS also documented a reduction in parasitemia among children under five from 43% to 28%; however, little or no improvement was noted for most of the other key indicators of progress (ITN ownership, ITN use, and antimalarial treatment) and IPTp uptake decreased from 60% in 2010 to 54% in 2012. As the 2012 MIS was completed prior to the 2012 ITN mass distribution campaign, 2012 MIS indicators for ITN ownership and use do not reflect the outcome of this campaign.

Despite the overall advances made since the initiation of PMI in Malawi, the MoH estimates that malaria still accounts for over a third of all outpatient visits with approximately 4.9 million suspected cases reported in 2012 (MoH, 2012). Additionally, malaria is the number one cause of hospital admissions among children under five, being responsible for about 40% of all hospitalizations in this age group (MOH, 2009). Approximately 98% of malaria cases are due to *Plasmodium falciparum.*

Other than PMI, the majority of the funding for malaria activities in Malawi comes from the Global Fund to Fight AIDS, Tuberculosis, and Malaria (Global Fund) and donor and government funds pooled through the health sector-wide approach (SWAp). The existing Global Fund grants focus on commodity procurement and distribution, including ITNs for routine and mass distribution and rapid diagnostic tests (RDTs) and artemisinin-based combination therapies (ACTs) for case management at the facility level, while pooled donor and government funds contribute to remaining malaria control activities. The Malawi malaria program was recently identified as an "interim applicant" during the Global Fund's transition to its new funding model. Malawi intends to use the vast majority of these funds to purchase injectable and rectal artesunate and second-line ACTs.

This FY 2014 PMI Malaria Operational Plan for Malawi was developed during a planning visit in July 2013 by representatives from the United States Agency for International Development (USAID), the US Centers for Disease Control and Prevention (CDC) and the Malawi NMCP. The proposed activities are aligned with Malawi's 2011-2015 Malaria National Strategic Plan. The FY 2014 MOP has been developed in close consultation with national and international partners involved with malaria control in Malawi and fills funding gaps from other major donors, while taking into account progress made to date. In addition to supporting efforts to control malaria, the team sought to increase integration with other GHI programs, and continue efforts to strengthen Malawi's health system. Based on these discussions and further meetings with the NMCP, the Plan proposes to support the activities outlined below. The total amount of PMI funding requested for Malawi in FY 2014 is $19,118,000.

Insecticide-Treated Nets: Malawi conducted a nationwide ITN mass distribution campaign between February and June 2012. The campaign complemented several years of consistent ITN distribution through routine systems (i.e., pregnant women at ANC visits and children less than five years old at their first immunization visit). According to the 2012 MIS, which was conducted several months prior to the completion of the mass distribution campaign, 55% of households owned one or more ITNs and 41% of the household population slept under an ITN the night before the survey. Among the high-risk groups, 56% of children under-five and 51% of pregnant women slept under an ITN the night before the survey. In households that own at least one ITN, 84% of children under five, and 79% of pregnant women slept under an ITN the night before the survey. In FY 2013, PMI distributed 900,000 ITNs to pregnant women and children under-five, complementing the quantity of ITNs procured through the Global Fund to provide complete coverage for the routine systems. An integrated behavior change communication program promoted universal ITN use throughout the year, along with promotion of care and repair of nets to extend their lifespan. With FY 2014 funding, PMI will procure 800,000 ITNs for free distribution through the routine systems to maintain high coverage of net ownership and use. Behavior change communication and community mobilization will be directed to promote appropriate ITN use and net care and repair. Support will also be provided to the NMCP for planning and logistics of the 2015 mass campaign.

Indoor Residual Spraying: In the first five years of PMI, Malawi expanded its IRS program from a pilot in part of Nkhotakota District to two full districts. Based on the success of the initial pilot, the MoH funded IRS activities in five additional districts in 2010. Nevertheless, Malawi's IRS activities have faced substantial challenges, including the emergence of pyrethroid resistance and technical problems that resulted in missed targets during the 2010 spray campaign. In FY 2011, given increased costs associated with an insecticide change to an organophosphate insecticide, PMI scaled back its direct support to IRS to Nkhotakota District to contain costs and maintain the quality of IRS activities. In FY 2012, PMI suspended direct support to IRS activities in Nkhotakota District because the increased cost (up to 15% of PMI budget) to protect just 3% of the population could not be justified within the current budget envelope without seriously jeopardizing other intervention areas of the PMI Malawi program. PMI did, however, continue to provide technical assistance for the GoM 2012-2013 spray campaign and ongoing entomological monitoring.

With FY 2013 funds, PMI will support the development of an integrated vector management strategy to determine the way forward for the IRS program. With FY 2014 funds, PMI will provide technical assistance to the NMCP to implement this evidence-based integrated vector management strategy. PMI will continue to support entomological monitoring, including mosquito resistance monitoring.

Malaria in Pregnancy: PMI, in collaboration with the NMCP, has helped achieved high rates of coverage nationally by strengthening focused antenatal care at the district and health facility level, procuring SP, and funding BCC efforts to encourage early and repeated ANC attendance. The 2012 MIS found that more than half (54%) of pregnant women received at least two doses of SP with at least one dose received during an antenatal care visit. However, the advent of *P. falciparum* resistance to SP is putting the effectiveness of the current IPTp strategy at risk and creating an urgent need to evaluate new drugs and approaches to reduce the burden of malaria in pregnancy. In line with World Health Organization guidance, PMI is collaborating with the NMCP and the Reproductive Health Unit to update the MOH policy to encourage the administration of SP at each scheduled ANC visit. With FY 2014 funding, PMI will continue to procure SP; emphasize supportive supervision of ANC services; encourage earlier attendance to ANC, especially among primigravidae; and monitor key *P. falciparum* resistance markers among pregnant women as well as evaluate SP resistance levels.

Case Management: In 2007, Malawi changed the first-line treatment for uncomplicated malaria from SP to the ACT artemether-lumefantrine (AL). To date, PMI has supported case management with AL at both the facility and community levels. In FY 2012, the NMCP updated the guidance for the treatment of severe malaria and now recommends use of parenteral artesunate at both hospital and health center levels. Artesunate is recommended for pre-referral treatment at the community level. With FY 2012 and FY 2013 funding, PMI is supporting the roll-out of these new policies through the procurement of injectable artesunate and training of health workers.

The 2011-2015 National Malaria Strategic Plan recommends diagnostic testing and treatment for all age groups at the community and facility levels. To achieve this goal, the NMCP has completed the roll-out of RDTs to the facility level and is currently piloting RDT use at the community level. PMI has provided substantial support to this RDT roll-out as well as the purchase of over 9 million RDTs in 2013. PMI also contributed to improving microscopy services.

Due to serious weaknesses within the Central Medical Stores (CMS), a temporary parallel supply chain was established in late 2010 to distribute Global Fund and USAID-procured health commodities directly to service delivery points. Implementing this privately managed supply chain has increased distribution costs, but the security and reliability of the system has greatly improved. PMI also contributes to strengthening the national supply chain so as to one day reintegrate all commodities with the CMS.

With FY 2014 funding, PMI plans to continue efforts to strengthen malaria case management at the facility and community levels, including the expansion of support for community case management to reach national coverage. PMI also plans to procure 3.3 million RDTs and 2 million ACTs to maintain prompt and effective treatment of malaria. Finally, PMI will continue to support the parallel supply chain and provide technical assistance to strengthen the public sector distribution network.

Monitoring and Evaluation: PMI's monitoring and evaluation activities are coordinated with the NMCP and other partners to share resources, ensure that critical gaps are being filled, and standardize data collection and reporting. PMI supported Malawi's second MIS in 2012. Additionally, PMI has provided funding for strengthening the national routine malaria information system; end-use verification surveys and service provision assessments; entomological monitoring; and health facility surveys to assess case management practices. Additionally, PMI is supporting operational research to assess the effectiveness of ITNs in an area with significant pyrethroid resistance as well as the use of cell phone technology to improve case management practices. Using FY 2013 funds, PMI will support the third MIS in 2014.

With FY 2014 funding, PMI will provide support for the 2015 Demographic Health Survey and continue to strengthen routine data collection; quarterly end- use verification surveys; entomologic monitoring; monitoring of key *Plasmodium falciparum* resistance markers among pregnant women and an evaluation of SP resistance levels to inform IPTp policy.

Behavior Change Communication: The National Malaria Strategic Plan calls for strengthening advocacy, communication, and social mobilization capacities to move towards universal coverage for all malaria interventions. The 2011-2014 Malaria Communication Strategy promotes an integrated approach to BCC to improve coverage of interventions targeting both health providers and community members. In 2013, PMI BCC implementing partners disseminated integrated and malaria specific messages through mass media campaigns throughout the country, completed formative research to tailor messages and inform future campaigns, built in-country capacity by training over 7,000 health personnel from the national to community level, provided public awareness of appropriate preventive behaviors through interpersonal community outreach activities to 2,790 community health leaders and to over 330,000 Malawians. In FY 2014, PMI plans to continue support to an integrated BCC approach at the national and community level for ITNs, IPTp, and case management. PMI will support malaria prevention activities targeting school-aged children as well as a small grants program for community-based organizations to support malaria prevention and control messaging. PMI will support the revision of the Malaria Communication Strategy to align it with the 2011-16 Health Sector Strategic Plan of the Ministry of Health.

Health Systems Strengthening and Capacity Building: In Malawi, PMI has increased its efforts to strengthen health systems while integrating with other United States Government programs to build capacity and improve outcomes. With FY 2014 funding, PMI will work with other USG health programs to enhance infrastructure, improve health information systems, strengthen financial management and provide support to the NMCP. PMI will also work with the Peace Corps office in Malawi to identify two or three Peace Corps volunteers to work with the NMCP.

STRATEGY

1. Introduction

Global Health Initiative

Malaria prevention and control is a major foreign assistance objective of the U.S. Government (USG). In May 2009, President Barack Obama announced the Global Health Initiative (GHI), a six-year, comprehensive effort to reduce the burden of disease and promote healthy communities and families around the world. Through the GHI, the United States will invest $63 billion over six years to help partner countries improve health outcomes, with a particular focus on improving the health of women, newborns and children. The GHI is a global commitment to invest in healthy and productive lives, building upon and expanding the USG's successes in addressing specific diseases and issues.

The GHI aims to maximize the impact the United States achieves for every health dollar it invests, in a sustainable way. The GHI's business model is based on: implementing a woman and girl-centered approach; increasing impact and efficiency through strategic coordination and programmatic integration; strengthening and leveraging key partnerships, multilateral organizations, and private contributions; encouraging country ownership and investing in country-led plans and health systems; improving metrics, monitoring and evaluation; and promoting research and innovation. The GHI will build on the USG's accomplishments in global health, accelerating progress in health delivery and investing in a more lasting and shared approach through the strengthening of health systems. Framed within the larger context of the GHI and consistent with the GHI's overall principles and planning processes, BEST (Best practices at scale in the home, community and facilities) is a USAID planning and review process that draws on our best experience in Family Planning, Mother and Child Health, and Nutrition to base our programs on the best practices to achieve the best impact.

President's Malaria Initiative

The President's Malaria Initiative (PMI) is a core component of the GHI, along with HIV/AIDS and tuberculosis. PMI was launched in June 2005 as a five-year, $1.2 billion initiative to rapidly scale up malaria prevention and treatment interventions and reduce malaria-related mortality by 50% in 15 high-burden countries in sub-Saharan Africa. With passage of the 2008 Lantos-Hyde Act, funding for PMI has now been extended through fiscal year (FY) 2014 and, as part of the GHI, the goal of PMI has been adjusted to reduce malaria-related mortality by 70% in the original 15 countries by the end of 2015. This will be achieved by continuing to scale up coverage of the most vulnerable groups — children under five years of age and pregnant women — with proven preventive and therapeutic interventions, including artemisinin-based combination therapies (ACTs), insecticide-treated nets (ITNs), intermittent preventive treatment of pregnant women (IPTp), and indoor residual spraying (IRS).

Malawi was selected as a PMI country in FY 2006. Large-scale implementation of ACTs and IPTp began in 2007 and has progressed rapidly with support from PMI and other partners. Artemisinin-based combination therapies and sulfadoxine-pyrimethamine (SP) for IPTp are now available and being used in all public health facilities nationwide. More than four million long-lasting ITNs have been distributed through routine systems to pregnant women and children under one year of age in the last three years, and a further 5.4 million ITNs were distributed throughout the country in a mass distribution campaign in 2012.

This FY 2014 Malaria Operational Plan (MOP) presents a detailed implementation plan for PMI in Malawi, based on the PMI Multi-Year Strategy and Plan and the National Malaria Control Program's (NMCP) 2011-2015 Malaria Strategic Plan. It was developed in consultation with the NMCP and with participation of national and international partners involved with malaria prevention and control in the country. The activities that PMI is proposing to support complement and sustain the National Malaria Strategic Plan and build on investments made by PMI and other partners to improve and expand malaria-related activities, including the Global Fund to Fight AIDS, Tuberculosis, and Malaria (Global Fund) malaria grants. This document briefly reviews the current status of malaria control policies and interventions in Malawi, describes progress to date, identifies challenges and unmet needs if the targets of the NMCP and PMI are to be achieved, and provides a description of planned FY 2014 activities.

2. Malaria Situation in Malawi

Malawi is a landlocked country bordered by Tanzania to the north, Zambia to the west, and Mozambique to the east and south. The population in 2014 is projected to be 15.8 million, comprised of approximately 51% women and 19% children less than five years old (National Statistical Office of Malawi).

Malaria is endemic in more than 95% of the country. Transmission is perennial in most areas and peaks after the start of the annual rains that typically begin in November-December and last through March-April in most parts of the country. The highest transmission areas are found along the hotter, wetter, and more humid low-lying areas (lakeshore, Shire River Valley, and central plain), while the lowest risk areas fall along the highland areas of Rumphi, Mzimba, Chitipa, and Kirk Range (Kazembe, 2006). *Anopheles funestus* is considered to be the primary vector species; *An. gambiae* s.s. and *An. arabiensis* also are present and may predominate in some areas at certain times of the year. *Plasmodium falciparum* is the most common species of malaria, accounting for 98% of the infections and almost all severe disease and deaths.

Figure 1. Predicted *Plasmodium falciparum* parasite prevalence in children under five years of age—Malawi, 2009–2010[1] (Figure by Adam Bennett, Tulane University)

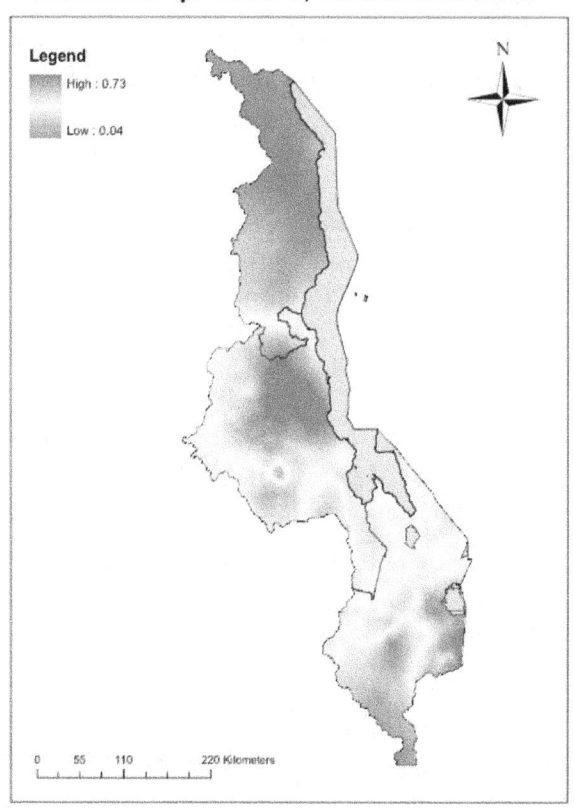

Predicted Pfpr under 5, Malawi 2009-2010

Malaria continues to be a major public health problem in Malawi. With approximately five million suspected cases annually, malaria is responsible for about 40% of all hospitalizations of children less than five years old and 30% of all outpatient visits across all ages. According to the 2012 Malaria Indicator Survey (MIS), among children under five years, malaria parasite prevalence by microscopy was 28% nationally.

Pregnant women and their fetuses are at high risk of the negative consequences of malaria. From 1996-2007, the incidence of placental malaria fell from 25% to 7% at the main referral hospital in Blantyre (Feng, 2010). Although this is a selected population with unusually easy access to the best medical services available in the public sector in Malawi, a similar low level of placental

[1] Survey data from the 2010 Malaria Indicator Survey (MIS) and 2009 Malaria Alert Center (MAC) anemia and parasitemia surveys were used to produce a predictive map of mean parasite prevalence for children aged less than five years in 2009 and 2010. A multivariate model was built using a Bayesian framework and included population size, altitude, land use, rainfall, age and survey year. Mean prevalence for the prediction model was 12.5% for Northern Region, 41% for Central Region, and 31% for Southern Region. These represent high-transmission season prevalence estimates.

malaria (5%) was measured in a rural area in Machinga District that was evaluated as part of a study monitoring the continued effectiveness of SP (Gutman, 2013).

Resistance of anopheline vectors to insecticides has been documented extensively in Malawi. In 2002, bioassays demonstrated that *An. arabiensis* was susceptible to pyrethroids and organophosphates but exhibited reduced susceptibility to dichloro-diphenyl-trichloroethane (DDT) (Mzilahowa, 2008). In 2009, resistance of *An. funestus* to pyrethroids and the carbamate insecticide bendiocarb was reported in Nkhotakota District, where a pilot IRS program had been implemented (Mzilahowa, personal communication) and on Likoma Island, situated on Lake Malawi (Hunt, 2010). Pyrethroid IRS was stopped in Nkhotakota and replaced with an organophosphate, which was sprayed for two years. Since then, pyrethroid and carbamate resistance in both IRS and non-IRS districts has been documented, limiting the options for IRS and causing concern about the continued effectiveness of ITNs.

3. Health System Delivery Structure and Ministry of Health Organization

The Malawi health service delivery system is pyramidal, consisting of tertiary, secondary, primary, and community care levels. District and central hospitals provide secondary and tertiary care services, respectively. Primary care is delivered through clinics and health centers where curative, maternity, and preventive services are offered. Rural populations' access to health facilities is generally good. Accessibility within a five-kilometer radius is estimated at 54%. Malawi also has more than 3,500 village health clinics (VHCs) in hard-to-reach areas as part of the community case management program (CCM). The CCM program is implemented by community-based health care workers (health surveillance assistants [HSAs]) who are trained to assess, classify, and provide first-line treatment for selected childhood illnesses in addition to referral to the next level of care. Local community-based organizations (CBOs) also provide non-clinical malaria services such as behavior change communication (BCC) on key malaria messages, counseling, and net distribution. The Malawi health system is highly decentralized with many programming decisions made at the district level. The Christian Health Association of Malawi (CHAM) operates health facilities mainly in rural areas nationwide and charges fees for the Essential Health Package (EHP) of services where service level agreements with the government have not been established.

The NMCP is located under the Ministry of Health's (MoH) Directorate of Preventive Health Services. The NMCP Program Manager is thus the Deputy Director of Preventive Health Services. In recent years, the program has expanded and now incorporates a core group of 12 technical officers, including an M&E position supported by PMI. The NMCP sets policies, establishes strategies, coordinates activities, and provides technical guidance for the MoH with respect to malaria prevention and control interventions. The management structure is comprised of 28 district malaria coordinators to direct activities in each district, 28 ITN coordinators, and seven IRS coordinators in the seven districts where IRS has been conducted.

4. Malaria Control Strategy in Malawi

The 2011-2015 National Malaria Strategic Plan, entitled "Towards Universal Access," builds on the successes achieved and lessons learned during implementation of the previous two strategic plans. The Malaria Strategic Plan was developed and approved by the MoH in early 2011; however, the NMCP has plans to align the Malaria Strategic Plan with the GoM's 2011-2016 Health Sector Strategic Plan (HSSP). Within the Malaria Strategic Plan, Malawi aims to move from targeting malaria control interventions to provision of universal access of proven interventions under which all Malawians at risk of malaria should have equitable access to malaria prevention, care and treatment. The NMCP activities are designed to be implemented within the HSSP and the Sector-Wide Approach (SWAp), including the provision of the essential health package. Specifically, the Malaria Strategic Plan objectives aim to ensure that the MoH through the NMCP is in a position to:

- Achieve universal coverage of all interventions by 2015 with an 80% utilization rate of the interventions;
- Strengthen advocacy, communication, and social mobilization capacities for malaria control by 2015 to improve use and adherence;
- Strengthen surveillance and M&E systems, including operational research for tracking progress in the implementation of malaria control activities by 2015;
- Strengthen capacity in program management to achieve malaria program objectives at all levels of health service delivery.

Within the Malaria Strategic Plan, six primary intervention areas are targeted: integrated vector management (IVM); case management; malaria in pregnancy; social mobilization and advocacy; surveillance, monitoring, evaluation and operations research; and program management.

IVM/ITNs: Malawi adopted an ITN policy in 2006 that includes free distribution of ITNs for children born in health facilities, children attending their first visit under the Expanded Program on Immunization (EPI) (if an ITN was not received at birth), and to pregnant women at their first visit to an antenatal care (ANC) clinic. The policy supports time-limited, national, free distribution campaigns that are conducted every two to three years. In February 2008, this policy was amended to include distribution to all children under five-years during their first visit to a health facility. Malawi aims to achieve universal coverage with ITNs, defined as one net for every two people, with the objective of increasing net ownership to 90% and net usage to 80% by 2015.

IVM/IRS: With the Malaria Strategic Plan, Malawi intends to expand IRS to 12 highly endemic districts through public, private sector, and community partnerships by 2015. With the emergence and expansion of insecticide resistance and the reduced effectiveness of IRS, the NMCP would like to use an evidence-based insecticide resistance management strategy to guide future vector control activities and entomologic monitoring.

Case management: The primary focus of the Malaria Strategic Plan includes expansion of parasitological confirmation of malaria through the use of microscopy in central and district hospitals as well as in facilities with high patient loads. The phased roll-out of rapid diagnostic tests (RDTs) to all health facilities began in November 2011, with a goal of expansion to community levels towards the end of 2013. The NMCP will scale up microscopy services at selected health facilities and district hospitals though trainings and procurement of microscopes with Global Fund support. The new treatment guidelines recommend that all children under five and pregnant women with fever be tested for malaria using an RDT.

In 2006, the MoH selected artemether-lumefantrine (AL) as the first-line drug for the treatment of uncomplicated malaria and artesunate-amodiaquine (ASAQ) as the second-line ACT, reserving parenteral quinine for the treatment of severe malaria and oral quinine for the management of malaria in the first trimester of pregnancy. The MoH has just finalized revising the guidelines for the management of severe malaria that recommend parenteral artesunate as the treatment for severe malaria at health facility and hospital levels and rectal artesunate as pre-referral treatment at community level. The MoH now is working to expand the availability of ACTs to the community through CCM with a focus on the approximately 3,500 hard-to-reach village health clinics.

Malaria in pregnancy: As part of a comprehensive focused ANC (FANC) package, Malawi's policy on IPTp is being revised. The new policy recommends administration of SP under directly observed therapy at each scheduled FANC visit after 16 gestational weeks. SP can be administered up to the time of delivery without safety concerns. Malawi is also developing guidelines and training manuals for the implementation of the policy, as well as alternative treatment for malaria in the first trimester of pregnancy, and prevention and management of anemia during pregnancy.

Social mobilization and advocacy: The Strategic Plan (and the 2009-2014 Malaria Communication Strategy) recommends social mobilization and advocacy strategies to increase the use of all malaria interventions through increased efforts aimed at qualitative and quantitative research, prioritization for promotion of targeted positive behaviors, and capacity building with an emphasis on the role of political and local leaders.

Surveillance, monitoring and evaluation, and operations research: With the Strategic Plan, the NMCP aims to strengthen routine data systems, surveillance, and operations research, promoting use of information while strengthening capacities for data use at all levels. The NMCP is working closely with Central Monitoring and Evaluation Department to incorporate core malaria indicators into the district health information system (DHIS 2). The 2011-2015 Monitoring and Evaluation Plan outlines the strategic areas to emphasize and focuses on tracking progress and measuring results of the various malaria prevention and control interventions to better inform policy, planning, and decision making.

Program management: The Strategic Plan also emphasizes capacity strengthening in program management at all levels of health service delivery. This requires resource mobilization and strengthened coordination across partners. The NMCP has linked its management objectives to existing national and international development strategies to enhance its policy direction. The procurement and supply chain management system was highlighted as an area requiring significant strengthening for program progress.

5. Integration, Collaboration, and Coordination

Malawi has been selected as one of a subset of countries for GHI's initial focus. To operationalize GHI, the USG health team in Malawi prioritizes close harmonization and communication internally across its agencies and disciplines, and externally with GoM and partners, both local and international. The State Department will coordinate this effort among in-country agencies including USAID, Health and Human Services/CDC, Department of Defense, and Peace Corps, as well as other USG agencies with potential contributions to GHI, but without in-country presence. Lessons learned from successful business models will improve efficiencies in coordination and implementation within USG, as well as with GoM and all partners. To ensure USG health programs are effectively aligned and coordinated with the priorities and efforts of Malawi's national health strategies and reports on health targets, the team strives to include Malawian leadership in the development and selection phase of various types of funding opportunities.

Malawi has identified three key areas where it focuses its GHI efforts:

- Enhancing leadership, governance, management, and accountability: In this area, specific interventions are identified to ensure demonstrable health leadership outcomes by the GoM. Combinations of interventions are undertaken, including performance-based financing, professional academic and mentor-based training, leadership and management training, and technical support for organizational development in key government ministries. This multi-pronged approach improves the health programs developed at the central level, and the quality of those programs implemented at district and facility levels both in terms of the services that are provided and the commodities that are procured and distributed.

- Improving human resources for health: USG supports the MoH to provide sustained and sufficient human resources and the equitable distribution of these workers; increase access to community health services; produce highly motivated and skilled staff whose performance is improved; and develop and approve key government policies impacting salaries, resources, and task-shifting. The strategic deployment of better-trained staff across districts and increased incentives for provision of quality services, in combination with strengthened quality improvement mechanisms, is expected to improve the community's confidence in the public health care system.

- Addressing health infrastructure deficiencies: Upgrades of facilities improve the accessibility of labor and delivery services in hard-to-reach communities and increase the accessibility of essential laboratory and other support services. Improved health information management allows clinics to better manage patient information and better layouts ensure integrated services are available at all facilities. These efforts are strengthened through renovations and maintenance of both ANC and labor and delivery settings to improve patient experiences and outcomes. We expect these enhancements to improve attendance and retention of staff in maternal and child health services.

In Malawi, the SWAp is the primary structure used to manage the health sector inputs. The SWAp is governed by a secretariat supported by technical working groups, which engage government and development partners to provide technical guidance and decision-making on key technical issues to the SWAp and ultimately the MoH. Development partners are also engaged in the SWAp governance structures through the Health Donor Group.

Malawi has three approved grants from the Global Fund, all of which designate the MoH as the Principal Recipient. The consolidated Rounds Two and Seven grants are in Phase Two and will end December 2013. The Round Nine grant entered Phase Two in January 2013 and will provide funding through December 2015. The Global Fund grants focus on procurement and distribution of ITNs for routine and mass distribution and RDTs and AL for case management at the facility and community levels. The Round Nine Phase One grant funded the 2012 ITN mass distribution campaign and the roll out of RDTs. The Round Nine Phase Two funding is targeted for a follow-up ITN mass campaign in 2015 and additional RDTs and ACTs. In February 2013, the Global Fund named the Malawi malaria program as an "interim applicant" during the Global Fund's transition to its new funding model. As such, Malawi will receive an additional $5 million during the 2013-2014 period. The Principal Recipient plans to use the funding to purchase injectable artesunate and rectal artesunate in line with WHO recommendations for the treatment of severe malaria at facility and community levels and ASAQ as second line treatment. A small amount will support strengthening M&E systems.

Table 1. Global Fund Malaria Grants in Malawi

Round	Phase 1 Amounts	Five-year funding maximum
2	$17,957,714	$44,706,715
7	$36,545,312	(combined)
2 & 7 (consolidated)	$54,503,026	$99,209,471
9	$28,032,760	$91,945,450
Interim Applicant (New Funding Model)	$5,000,000	$5,000,000 (pending approval)
Total	$82,535,786	$191,154,921

The NMCP also receives technical assistance from the United Nations Children's Fund (UNICEF) to support programmatic management, malaria prevention and control efforts at the district level, and development of BCC materials. The World Health Organization (WHO) also provides assistance on a variety of technical issues.

Other key partners in Malawi include the United Kingdom Department for International Development (DfID), which provides sector budget support, which includes support for NMCP, and procures "essential medicine kits." The Clinton Health Access Initiative (CHAI) promotes the use of injectable artesunate as the first-line treatment for severe malaria. In this capacity, CHAI serves as the in country implementer of the UNITAID grant to Medicines for Malaria Venture to purchase injectable artesunate. The CHAI is also supporting community case management in four districts (Mzimba North, Ntcheu, Ntchisi and Dedza).

Within the USG
Malawi is a President's Emergency Plan for AIDS Relief (PEPFAR) focus country, receiving $75 million in FY 2013 for the prevention, care, and treatment of HIV/AIDS. PEPFAR and PMI share several implementation partners working on integrated or common platforms to support improved health outcomes in Malawi. The PMI team works closely with PEPFAR and the USAID health teams to coordinate activities.

6. PMI Goals, Targets, and Indicators

The goal of PMI is to reduce malaria-associated mortality by 70% compared to pre-initiative levels in the 15 original PMI countries by the end of 2015. PMI will also assist Malawi to achieve the following targets in populations at risk for malaria:

- >90% of households with a pregnant woman and/or children under five will own at least one ITN;
- 85% of children under five will have slept under an ITN the previous night;
- 85% of pregnant women will have slept under an ITN the previous night;
- 85% of houses in geographic areas targeted for IRS will have been sprayed;

- 85% of pregnant women and children under five will have slept under an ITN the previous night or in a house that has been sprayed with IRS in the past six months;
- 85% of women who have completed a pregnancy in the last two years will have received two or more doses of IPTp during that pregnancy;
- 85% of government health facilities have ACTs available for treatment of uncomplicated malaria; and
- 85% of children under five with suspected malaria will have received treatment with ACTs within 24 hours of onset of their symptoms.

7. Progress on Indicators to Date

The most up-to-date information on the status of malaria prevention and control interventions in Malawi comes from the 2012 MIS and 2010 DHS. The table below shows progress since the 2006 Multiple Indicator Cluster Survey (MICS). It should be noted that the 2012 MIS was completed prior to the 2012 ITN mass distribution campaign, and indicators for net ownership and use do not reflect the outcome of this campaign.

Table 2. Progress on Indicators to Date

Indicator	MICS 2006	MIS 2010	DHS 2010	MIS 2012
Percentage of households that own one or more ITNs	38	58	57	55
Percentage of children less than five years old who slept under an ITN the previous night	25	55	38	56
Percentage of pregnant women who slept under an ITN the previous night	8	49	35	51
Percentage of children less than five years old with fever in the last two weeks who received an appropriate antimalarial drug	24	31	43	33
Percentage of children less than five years old who took an antimalarial drug the same or next day	N/A	22	28	24
Percentage of pregnant women who took two or more doses of IPTp during their last pregnancy	48	60	55	54
Prevalence of malaria parasitemia by slide microscopy	N/A	43%	N/A	28%

8. Other Relevant Evidence on Progress

PMI Malawi has supported two national health facility surveys to assess the status of case management of malaria in public health facilities. The first was conducted in 2011 (prior to the national roll-out of RDTs to health facilities) and focused on the management of uncomplicated malaria. In total, 107 health facilities, 2,019 outpatients, and 135 health workers were surveyed. Key findings include:

- Thirty-four percent of all patients seeking curative care at outpatient departments during the high-transmission season had parasitologically-confirmed, uncomplicated malaria.

- Sixty-seven percent of patients with malaria confirmed by microscopy were correctly treated with an ACT and correct dosing of ACTs was high (95%). The main cause of incorrect treatment was malaria cases missed by clinicians (27% of patients with malaria were not diagnosed with malaria).

- Thirty-one percent of patients without malaria received an ACT. Among patients with negative microscopy results, 22% were nevertheless prescribed AL.

- Access to malaria diagnostics was insufficient and only 42% of patients attended facilities with functional microscopy. The quality of facility microscopy was poor compared to expert microscopists (sensitivity = 47% and specificity = 84%).

- Most patients were seen by health workers (69%) explicitly trained on the malaria treatment guidelines. Eighty-four percent of patients were seen by health workers trained on malaria case management guidelines.

The second national health facility survey was conducted in 2012 and focused on the management of severe malaria. In total, 200 health workers were surveyed at 36 hospitals that admit patients with severe malaria and 1,252 inpatient records were reviewed. Key findings include:

- Although 42% of patients were given an admission diagnosis of malaria, 76% of all severe malaria patients received intravenous quinine, the first-line medication for the treatment of severe malaria. Sixty-five percent of patients had parasitologic confirmation of their diagnosis on admission.

- Quinine was available in 92% of the hospitals on the day of the survey, but 26% of facilities reported at least one stockout of all severe malaria treatments within the prior three months. RDTs were available in 97% of the facilities, but were out of stock at least once in the prior three months in 44% of facilities. Microscopy supplies were available in 89% of the facilities, but out of stock in 22% of facilities in the prior three months.

- On the job malaria training was reported by 57% of health workers, primarily on the use of RDTs. Only 5% reported malaria supervision in the prior six months.

- Slightly more than half (57%) of health workers were able to name at least three signs of severe malaria, and 74% knew the correct treatment of severe malaria in a two-year old. Seventy-four percent knew how to treat a person with fever and a negative RDT result.

- Health workers cited availability of treatment (58%), availability of diagnostic supplies (32%), and knowledge gaps (30%) as the main obstacles to malaria care.

With funding and support from PMI, Malawi and the RBM partnership completed an impact evaluation of malaria control efforts between 2000 and 2010. The *Progress and Impact Series* report was launched in April 2013. Key findings included a 41% reduction in under-five mortality from 188 to 112 deaths per 1000 live births over the period 1996-2000 and 2006-2010, and modeling, which estimated that approximately 21,600 deaths among children under five-years of age were prevented by malaria control interventions.

9. Challenges, Opportunities, and Threats

Malawi's malaria program has reached a critical juncture with several threats to its success including: 1) continued supply chain problems; 2) the conclusion of the current Global Fund malaria grants; 3) lack of an evidence-based IVM strategy in the face of insecticide resistance, which threatens the IRS program and potentially the ITN program; 4) increased resistance to SP, which threatens the effectiveness of the IPTp program; 5) unreliable malaria data from the HMIS resulting in program monitoring challenges; and 6) an under-trained and under-supervised health workforce, which limit improvements to the health care delivery system in Malawi.

Since PMI began work in Malawi, supply chain issues have plagued the program. Stockouts of antimalarials and other essential drugs have occurred regularly due to issues related to quantification of need, ordering, tendering, receipt, storage, and the logistics of distribution. Beginning in 2007, PMI distributed its ACTs through the Central Medical Stores Trust (CMS), under the stipulation that CMS improve its storage facilities, documentation and information management system, transportation capacity, security, and logistics management system. Many of these changes did not materialize and difficulties in record keeping, data management, warehousing, and commodity tracking continued to prevent the development of a strong supply chain, both within CMS and the MoH.

In mid-2010, PMI became aware of significant thefts of PMI-procured antimalarial drugs from CMS, resulting in the USG withdrawing its funded commodities from CMS and establishing a temporary parallel supply chain for the distribution of PMI-procured health commodities and family planning commodities directly to service delivery points. Of late, improved implementation of this parallel system has resulted in less frequent stockouts of antimalarial commodities. However, a weak logistics management information system (LMIS) and irregular procurements and deliveries of commodities continue to limit the ability of this system to accurately forecast commodity needs and ensure availability of the commodities at the point of service.

Vector control faces its own challenges, primarily related to the emergence and expansion of insecticide resistance to pyrethroids and carbamates. This caused the PMI-supported IRS program change to a more expensive and short-acting organophosphate insecticide, which ultimately made the IRS program unsustainable within the existing budget envelope. Currently, PMI is working with the MoH and other partners to determine the most appropriate way forward for Malawi's IRS program. The impact of pyrethroid resistance on the effectiveness of ITNs is unknown and PMI is supporting research to answer that question and to evaluate third generation/new combination ITNs that could potentially mitigate the effects of resistance.

Results from recent studies in Malawi suggest increasing levels of SP resistance among pregnant women attending ANC and limited effects on birth outcomes among women receiving IPTp with SP. Given the current lack of a viable alternative to SP for IPTp, these findings represent a serious threat to the current and future effectiveness of the IPTp program in Malawi.

Routine monitoring of malaria indicators through the HMIS remains a challenge and poor data quality continues to limit the ability of the MoH to make evidenced-based programmatic decisions. Nevertheless, progress on data collection is being made, especially the scale-up to all districts of the DHIS 2. Although in its infancy in Malawi, the use of electronic medical record systems holds promise for the future and may present a platform for malaria surveillance and program monitoring.

Finally, the country overall has been plagued with major human resource issues that have resulted in a reliance upon health workers with lower levels of training for the performance of key malaria prevention and case management activities. Providing adequate support for training and supervision for this cadre of the health workforce has proved challenging, as much of the PMI support for case management activities (training and supervision for CCM) has been channeled through an integrated service delivery platform targeted to only 15 of the 29 districts. This has left a gap in support in the remaining districts that has been filled only partially by other development partners and agencies.

On a positive note, the President of Malawi continues to show strong commitment to improving health and supporting the health sector. Such political will may result in increased GoM resources dedicated to health, as well as potential increased donor support.

10. PMI Support Strategy

PMI's strategy is to support the NMCP's malaria control and prevention efforts. PMI is committed to ensuring high net ownership and use by continuing to support the procurement and distribution of ITNs through routine systems at ANC and EPI clinics in addition to providing logistical support for universal coverage campaigns. The routine distribution system is well established and has been effective at ensuring that nets are available to these vulnerable populations. Following the universal coverage campaign in 2015, PMI will support a survey to understand the campaign's reach and impact by evaluating net ownership and use. PMI will explore other channels to provide ITNs on a continuous basis to provide more opportunities to increase the number of nets in each household.

Although PMI recognizes IRS as a key malaria prevention strategy, the documented pyrethroid resistance and high cost of alternative insecticides have increased IRS program costs to approximately 15% of the total PMI budget. Considering these facts, the PMI team does not believe that continued spraying can be justified within the current budget without seriously jeopardizing other intervention areas of the PMI Malawi program. PMI will work with the NMCP to design an evidence-based insecticide resistance management strategy to guide future vector control activities and entomologic monitoring.

Intermittent preventive treatment in pregnancy is one of the hallmarks of reducing the impact of malaria in Malawi. PMI is developing a protocol to monitor *P. falciparum* resistance to SP in pregnant women in Malawi in response to evidence that SP is becoming less effective within the IPTp program. Biomarker monitoring for resistance, in addition to an evaluation of SP for IPTp, will help to inform IPTp policy. PMI will undertake these operations research studies with FY 2014 funding.

At the facility and community levels, PMI is committed to ensuring that there is access to high quality malaria case management. To ensure that there is a consistent availability of commodities; PMI will maintain support to the parallel supply chain while providing technical assistance to improve the capacity of the CMS at the central level and strengthening the LMIS at the district level. PMI will continue to provide supportive supervision and training for the management of uncomplicated malaria in its focus districts as part of a broader maternal and child health effort. Additionally, PMI will support the NMCP's efforts to implement a new treatment policy for the management of severe malaria with parenteral artesunate in health facilities. At the community level, PMI will continue to work in the 15 designated districts to support HSAs providing CCM with training, commodities, and oversight for the use of RDTs and ACTs. Looking forward, PMI will work with the NMCP to expand the CCM program to include pre-referral rectal artesunate and RDTs. PMI will also continue to strengthen quality assurance for diagnostics, for both microscopy and RDTs, at the facility and community level.

All of these activities will be grounded in a strong monitoring and evaluation framework that includes both population-based surveys, operations research, review of HMIS data and other relevant activities. PMI will support the implementation of DHS every five years with an MIS survey in the intermediate years to determine progress against PMI and NMCP targets. This will be complemented by regular monitoring of HMIS data by the NMCP, treatment consumption data, entomological data, and other surveys such as health facility surveys and targeted operations research supported by PMI and other groups.

OPERATIONAL PLAN

1. Insecticide-Treated Nets

NMCP/PMI Objectives

The 2011-15 Malaria Strategic Plan calls for universal coverage with ITNs, defined as one net for every two people. The plan includes specific targets to increase household ITN ownership of at least one ITN to 90% of households and to achieve 80% ITN usage among all demographic groups. Malawi has a three-pronged strategy for ITN distribution: (1) free routine distribution through ANC to pregnant women and EPI clinics to children less than one year old,[2] (2) time-limited, intermittent mass campaigns to the general population, and (3) sale of subsidized ITN through the private sector to complement the free public sector distributions.

Progress in the last 12 months

Malawi conducted a nationwide ITN mass distribution campaign February-June 2012. Originally, the campaign was scheduled to occur towards the end of 2011 to coincide with the peak malaria season and the 2012 MIS data collection; however, due to logistical and programmatic challenges, the distribution of the ITNs did not start until the end of May 2012, except in districts supported by partners that started as early as the first week of February 2012. A total of 5.6 million ITNs were distributed across the country, although there was a shortfall of approximately 800,000 ITNs. The NMCP had planned to conduct a mop-up campaign shortly after the campaign ended; however, the mop-up campaign was also delayed as the ITNs did not arrive in Malawi until April 2013. The mop-up campaign is now projected for late 2013. The Global Fund will support the warehousing and distribution of these nets.

The NMCP had intended to conduct an ITN coverage survey nationwide within three months of the completion of the 2012 mass distribution campaign. Due to the gaps in net distribution and delay of the mop-up campaign, it was not considered feasible to conduct an accurate coverage survey. No formal evaluation of the 2012 mass distribution campaign has been undertaken.

The 2012 MIS was conducted several months prior to the mass distribution campaign, and does not take into account the impact of the campaign. Household ownership of at least one ITN, which had increased between 2006 and 2010 from 38% (MICS 2006) to 58% (MIS 2010), had not significantly changed by 2012, remaining at 55% (MIS 2012). This slight decrease in household ITN ownership was mirrored in the reduction in the household ownership of any mosquito net, whether treated or untreated, from 63% in 2010 to 60% in 2012, and in the decrease in the average number of nets per household of 1.0 in 2010 to 0.9 in 2012. The

---

[2] The 2011-15 Malaria Strategic Plan calls for free routine distribution through ANC to pregnant women and EPI clinics to children *less than five years old*; However, following the 2012 mass distribution campaign, the NMCP started targeting routine distribution to pregnant women and children *less than one year old*.

percentage of households with at least one ITN for every two persons, the target by which the success of the mass distribution campaign will be evaluated, was 19% (MIS 2012).

With the 2011-15 Malaria Strategic Plan and the 2012 mass distribution campaign, there was a change from targeting ITNs to only the most vulnerable groups (pregnant women and children less than five years old) to universal coverage of the general population. However, the 2010 MIS only collected ITN usage data on the vulnerable groups and women of reproductive age. In the 2010 MIS, the reported utilization of ITNs the night before the survey by children less than five years old, pregnant women and women of reproductive age was 55%, 49% and 51%, respectively. In 2012, the use among children less than five years old had increased to 61%, and use among pregnant women had increased slightly to 51% (MIS 2012). Although the 2012 MIS did not report information on women of reproductive age per se, use of ITNs was highest among persons aged 35-39 at 48%.

In households where at least one ITN was available, 84% of children less than five years old and 79% of pregnant women slept under an ITN the night before the survey (MIS 2012). Among the general population, usage among all age groups increased significantly in households with at least one ITN. This finding suggests that ITNs are used when available, and that the 2012 ITN mass distribution campaign could have increased significantly the overall utilization of ITNs – both in children less than five years old and the general population.

In light of increasing ITN coverage due to mass distributions and the routine system, the national mass media campaigns and print media have been modified to emphasize "every night" ITN use by all members of the household as well as proper care and repair of nets. The Malaria Alert Centre, in conjunction with CDC, is conducting a study of the longevity and durability of ITNs. These data are being analyzed and will be presented by the end of 2013.

PMI continues to fund community-based organizations and local NGOs through the sub-grants. These organizations are using community mobilization to increase awareness of ITNs, improve messaging about correct and consistent use, educate on proper care and repair, and conduct behavior change interventions through community-based activities.

PMI continues to work with the NMCP to enhance partnerships that exist between the NMCP and stakeholders and partners around ITN procurement and distribution. These partnerships have proved beneficial in enhancing the national strategic plan for malaria control.

Challenges, opportunities, and threats

The opportunity to significantly increase ITN coverage by distributing ITNs through a mass campaign has been achieved. The exact impact of the campaign has yet to be measured, but during a two-month period, more than 5.6 million ITNs were distributed in Malawi. High attendance rates for ANC and EPI visits mean that the routine system is able to reach high coverage of the target group. Use of ITNs by children under five is high in households with ITNs, suggesting that the recent mass distribution campaign could lead to significantly improved utilization of ITNs in this target group.

With the measurement of ITN use among all age groups in the 2012 MIS, it is apparent that older children and adolescents aged 5-14 have a much lower utilization of ITNs than other age groups. The proportion in this age group that slept under an ITN in Malawi was 30%, and in houses with at least one ITN it was 52%, much lower than in any other age group (MIS 2012). Older children and adolescents may not regularly use an ITN because of past prioritization of children less than five years old and pregnant women for ITNs, and because of the lack of designated sleeping spaces in many households for children in this age group. As malaria transmission declines, it is precisely children aged 5-14 years old who will bear the burden of malaria infection and, increasingly, clinical malaria. Strategies to improve ITN use among this age group should be identified and employed. BCC campaigns are being designed to target this age group with messages promoting use of ITNs.

Additional challenges to the ITN program include inconsistent reporting and record keeping at the health facility level; lack of priority on ITN issues in the HMIS; distribution planning not based on actual demand; lack of training for healthcare workers (including HSAs) on ITN reporting, messaging and targeting; and lack of a clear definition of the lifespan of ITNs in Malawi.

Another critical issue for the ITN program is the emergence of mosquito resistance to pyrethroid insecticides. It is not clear how much of a threat this presents to the continued effectiveness of ITNs. The NMCP, MAC and CDC are currently involved in research efforts to help understand the impact of pyrethroid resistance on ITN effectiveness and evaluate new combination ITNs that carry a synergist that can mitigate pyrethroid resistance.

Gap analysis

The table below shows the gap analysis, including assumptions used in calculating ITN needs for the routine systems and mass distribution, and distribution by partner for calendar years 2013-2015.

Table 3. Gap Analysis for ITNs

Calendar Year	2013	2014	2015
Total Population	**15,316,861**	**15,805,240**	**16,310,430**
Routine Distribution Needs			
Pregnant women during first prenatal care visit (5% of the population); assumes 100% attendance for one visit	765,843	790,262	815,522
Children under 1 (5% of the population) in all malarious areas through EPI clinics, assuming 100% EPI coverage	765,843	790,262	815,522
Estimated total need for routine channels	*1,531,686*	*1,580,524*	*1,631,044*
Mass Distribution Needs			
2015 mass distribution campaign throughout the country			9,061,350
2012 mass campaign mop-up	800,000		
Estimated total need for mass campaigns	*800,000*		*9,061,350*
Total Routine and Mass ITN Needs	**2,331,686**	**1,580,524**	**10,692,394**
Partner Contributions			
PMI (primarily routine channels)	501,000	900,000	800,000
Global Fund Rounds 2/7	800,000	1,479,666	
Global Fund Round 9 Phase 2			9,061,350
Private sector	25,000	40,000	
Total Partner Contributions	**1,326,000**	**2,419,666**	**9,861,350**
Carryover from previous year	**738,376**	**0**	**839,142**
Total ITNs available in calendar year	**2,064,376**	**2,419,666**	**10,700,492**
Surplus* (Gap)	**(267,310)**	**839,142**	**8,098**

*Surpluses are carried over into the next year, but deficits are not.

The need for ITNs for the routine system in 2015 is 1,631,044 ITNs. In 2014, the NMCP will procure 1,479,666 ITNs for the routine system using its Global Fund consolidated grant. This procurement will result in a surplus of 839,142 ITNs in 2014. This surplus will carry over into 2015. The Global Fund is expected to provide funding for the total number of ITNs needed for the mass distribution campaign in 2015. PMI will procure 800,000 ITNs with FY 2014 funds to supplement the net surplus from the Global Fund procurement to fully cover the routine distribution systems in 2015.

Planned activities with FY 2014 funding and justification

Malawi is planning for the next mass distribution campaign in 2015. Malawi continues to provide ITNs through the routine system to children less than one year old and pregnant women. PMI will focus on sustaining the routine distribution system. In addition, PMI will provide technical and logistical support to the 2015 mass distribution campaign.

Behavior change communication activities will be carried out through national level communication and the community-based small grants program to promote ITN use among all household members and to enhance net care and repair. Additionally, PMI will support development of malaria specific prevention messages and activities targeted at school-aged children (see BCC section).

Description and budget for proposed activities ($3,878,000)

- Procurement of 800,000 ITNs targeting pregnant women and children under one through the ANC and EPI free distribution ($2,872,000);
- Distribution of ITNs from the central level to the health facilities including customs clearing, warehousing, transport, distribution and ITN tracking at the health facility ($856,000);
- Technical and logistical support to the NMCP to plan for the 2015 mass distribution campaign, including a consultant for micro-planning, and supportive supervision during the campaign ($150,000).

2. Indoor Residual Spraying

NMCP/PMI objectives

The primary IRS objectives of the 2011-2015 Malaria Strategic Plan include: coverage of at least 85% of all targeted structures in 12 high transmission districts by 2015 through public, private sector and community partnerships; advocacy for the removal of taxes and tariffs of IRS commodities and supplies; and advocacy for more resources for IRS from government and external funders. IRS activities include planning and training, operational work, comprehensive monitoring and evaluation of spraying activities, environmental compliance and entomological monitoring and surveillance.

Progress in the last 12 months

In mid-2012, following careful review and consultations, PMI suspended direct support for IRS activities in Nkhotakota District. Increasing insecticide resistance in the district had led to a shift to a non-pyrethroid insecticide (Actellic EC), which increased the IRS costs to approximately 15% of the annual PMI budget. With only 3% of Malawi's total population protected by IRS for only two to three months of the year, the cost was considered too high for the small benefit received. In addition, high LLIN coverage levels had been achieved in Nkhotakota District through routine and mass distribution efforts, providing some assurance that the reduction in malaria transmission achieved with previous IRS campaigns would be maintained even in the absence of IRS.

In response to the suspension of IRS activities in Nkhotakota District, PMI and the NMCP collaborated to monitor any significant increases in cases of severe malaria and ensured that extra supplies of RDTs and ACTs were available for use in the district. To establish a baseline, PMI conducted, during the last quarter of 2012, a retrospective review of severe malaria cases in Nkhotakota District, which included the five-year period before IRS began (2002-2006) and the five-year period during which IRS was conducted (2007-2011). Following this review, PMI initiated prospective monitoring that will be implemented for at least the next two years. Notably, this monitoring did not show any problematic rise in severe malaria cases in Nkhotakota District after the suspension of IRS.

Although PMI suspended direct support for spray activities in 2012, support continued for entomological surveillance activities in the seven IRS districts during the 2012-2013 spray campaign carried out by the GoM. The major entomological activities included monitoring vector abundance, determining insecticide decay rates, and monitoring for insecticide resistance. Key results from the 2012-13 IRS spray campaign demonstrated the following:

- *An. funestus* was predominant in four districts (Nkhatabay, Nkhotakota, Salima and Chikwawa)

- *An. gambiae* was very common in Karonga prior to spraying.

- Alphacypermethrin used for IRS lasted for only a month on sprayed wall surfaces.

Although PMI did not provide direct support for spray activities during the 2012-2013 Malawi IRS campaign, technical assistance was provided to the NMCP for these activities. This support included: the development of IRS guidelines; training of national trainers to ensure standardization of IRS across all the implementation districts; pre-, mid- and post-spray environmental compliance inspections; and waste disposal.

The NMCP is considering conducting nationwide resistance mapping with non-PMI funds to better understand resistance patterns outside of the districts where PMI is already monitoring.

Challenges, opportunities, and threats

To date, Malawi has made steady progress in the scale-up of IRS activities, from a pilot program in 2007 to a regional program implemented in seven districts. However, IRS activities have encountered several challenges. Malaria transmission is high and perennial with a peak malaria transmission period of at least six months duration, longer than the residual effect of most insecticides. Entomological monitoring and surveillance has provided evidence of emergence and expansion of resistance of *An. funestus* to pyrethroids in most of the IRS implementation districts. For example, during the 2012-13 IRS spray period, *An. funestus* showed high levels of insecticide resistance to pyrethroids in both IRS and non-IRS districts: Nkhotakota (IRS district 19 – 46% mortality); Mwanza (non-IRS district 30 – 46.9%); Phalombe (non-IRS district

47.5%); Balaka (non-IRS district 7.6 – 66.7%); and Machinga (non-IRS district 41.3%). *An. funestus* was completely susceptible to Malathion™, an organophosphate.

Securing GoM funding and resources to support the implementation of IRS in the remaining six IRS targeted districts continues to be a challenge, as evidenced by the purchase of poor quality spray pumps and personal protective equipment, delayed logistics and scheduling, and poor maintenance of warehouses. As in previous IRS spray campaigns, the most recent campaign encountered several issues, including: inadequate supervision at the district level; inadequate storage facilities; difficulty adhering to the IRS spray schedule and environmental requirements; and difficulties disposing of waste resulting from the spray campaign.

The NMCP has recently come under pressure to consider the use of DDT in its IRS program. However, there is significant resistance from the agricultural industry, who fear that the use of DDT could result in an agricultural products export ban. Additionally, Malawi has not yet ratified the Stockholm Convention for the use of DDT for IRS. In view of these issues, the NMCP, in consultation with various stakeholders, is considering conducting a pilot of DDT spraying in Nkhotakota District. The absence of a comprehensive vector control strategy for the country, coupled with a lack of in-country technical capacity and resources to implement this pilot, make it unlikely that the NMCP could implement this pilot without external support.

Despite these challenges, the GoM continues to support IRS as one of the main strategies to reduce malaria transmission in high burden districts. Previous PMI-funded IRS efforts have substantially improved human resource capacity within the NMCP (two staff members are now dedicated to IRS activities) and in the current seven IRS-targeted districts. Additionally, several private sector institutions are implementing IRS on a smaller scale, which presents an opportunity to build partnerships and improve program sustainability.

Commodity gap analysis

The NMCP procured 2,000 spray pumps and 2,000 sets of personal protective equipment for spray operators during the scale-up period. The majorities of these pumps have developed faults and are causing environmental concerns due to leakages during spraying. With FY 2012 reprogramming funds, PMI procured and supported the NMCP with 980 sets of personal protective equipment and handed over 2,000 sets of personal protective equipment and 1,000 pumps as part of the close-out of the agreement with the PMI implementing partner. This should prove adequate for the coming spray season.

Planned activities with FY 2014 funding and justification

The future of the IRS program in Malawi is uncertain due to the resource challenges being experienced in the country. The GoM is prioritizing the execution of its health activities and it is unknown if IRS will remain a high priority intervention given the emergence and expansion of pyrethroid resistance and the recent LLIN mass distribution campaign.

Further, the emergence of pyrethroid resistance has made the implementation of IRS difficult, particularly in light of the high cost of organophosphates and the environmental concerns and costs associated with DDT. PMI will use FY 2013 funding to support the development of an integrated vector management plan. If a viable way forward is identified, PMI will use FY 2014 funding to provide technical assistance to the NMCP to implement the IRS component of this plan.

PMI will continue supporting entomological and insecticide resistance monitoring in sentinel sites. Although these sentinel sites have been located primarily in the seven districts where IRS activities have been conducted, PMI and the NMCP are reviewing the entomological monitoring strategy and will relocate some sites to better represent the distinct eco-epidemiological zones in Malawi.

Description and budget for proposed activities ($75,000)

- Technical assistance to the NMCP to implement an evidence-based integrated vector management strategy ($75,000);

- Continued support for entomologic monitoring with routine surveys of vector density and insecticide resistance testing of mosquitoes collected from sentinel villages in at least three districts (up to a total maximum of seven districts) where the NMCP is conducting IRS (see M&E section).

3. Malaria in Pregnancy
NMCP/PMI objectives

Historically, Malawi has played an important role in the development of IPTp policy and continues to be one of the countries with the highest rate of IPTp coverage. The MoH has a three-pronged approach to reducing the burden of malaria in pregnancy: use of IPTp, LLINs, and effective case management of malarial illness and anemia. PMI supports this approach for malaria in pregnancy implemented through the antenatal care services delivery platform. The MoH is in the process of updating the national policy on IPTp to reflect the new WHO guidelines. The draft malaria in pregnancy guidelines for Malawi recommend that "all pregnant women with no signs of clinical malaria whose pregnancies are 16 gestational weeks and above should be given SP at each scheduled antenatal care visit" (GoM 2013). The doses should be administered at least four weeks apart and given as directly observed therapy. The last dose of SP can be administered safely up to delivery. The MoH's objective for IPTp is for at least 80% of pregnant women to receive at least three doses of SP during pregnancy. This objective is to be accomplished through a partnership with the Reproductive Health Unit (RHU) to provide directly observed IPTp during focused antenatal care visits at least three times during pregnancy. In addition, behavior change messages are communicated at ANC visits and at the community level to retain demand for IPTp. LLINs are provided to pregnant women at their first ANC visit.

Country/PMI progress in the last 12 months

PMI, in conjunction with the NMCP and RHU, has worked to increase uptake of IPTp through training of providers and assistance with directly observed treatment, including supporting infrastructure improvements to assure clean water supply and provision of cups. Additionally, PMI provided funds to update the IPTp policy targeted at improving the uptake of IPTp and allowing women visiting ANC later in their pregnancy to take three or more doses of SP. Through CBOs and the small grants program, funds have been made available at the local level to increase demand for IPTp services. Specifically, community-based messages help increase demand for ANC and IPTp and encourage women to attend ANC early in their pregnancy to receive at least three doses of SP. These messages are being delivered as part of an integrated package addressing all malaria interventions. PMI also supports communications campaigns at the national level using radio and other mass media channels.

The 2012 MIS found that more than half (54%) of pregnant women received IPTp, that is, at least two doses of SP with at least one dose received during an antenatal care visit, which occurred during the most recent pregnancy. This percentage is a slight decline from the 2010 MIS (60%). Additionally, this percentage is below the 80% goal set by the MoH. Awareness campaigns and provision of LLINs through ANC clinics support the use of LLINs during pregnancy. In the 2012 MIS, 51% of pregnant women reported sleeping under an ITN the night before. This goal is also well below the 80% coverage level set by the MoH.

The malaria in pregnancy guidelines recommend the use of iron and folic acid supplementation for the treatment of anemia during pregnancy. Folic acid at levels of 5mg or higher are known to reduce the efficacy of SP as antimalarial medicine. Thus, to safeguard SP's efficacy, PMI promotes procurement of folic acid of 400 micrograms. Currently, the MoH procures 400 micrograms folic acid tablets through the Reproductive Health Unit's essential drug program.

For uncomplicated malaria, the treatment guidelines recommend that during the first trimester, quinine be administered for seven days. In the second and third trimesters of pregnancy, an AL is recommended. For the treatment of severe malaria during the first trimester of pregnancy, the treatment guidelines recommend parenteral quinine for at least 24 hours. When the patient is able to take oral medication, quinine is then given to complete the treatment. In the second and third trimesters of pregnancy, parenteral artesunate is recommended for at least 24 hours, followed by AL once the patient is able to take oral medication. Because the WHO recommends combination treatment regimens to reduce the probability of drug resistance developing, the GoM is in the process of updating the treatment guidelines for malaria in pregnancy to include clindamycin with quinine treatment during the first trimester of pregnancy for uncomplicated and severe malaria.

Challenges, opportunities, and threats

Despite high first attendance at ANC clinics (90%), IPTp goals in Malawi have not yet been met.

Although the integration of IPTp into focused ANC services helps assure that IPTp is available in all health centers and administered by trained personnel, there is potentially some dilution of impact, as IPTp is one among many services offered at ANC.

One significant threat to IPTp in Malawi is the evidence of increasing SP resistance. In 2012, more than 94% of the malaria parasites in pregnant women with asymptomatic parasitemia presenting at an ANC visit at Machinga District Hospital had quintuple mutations for SP resistance, indicating that resistance is almost fixed in this population (Mwandama D, personal communication, 2012). The PCR-corrected day 42 treatment efficacy for SP to cure asymptomatic parasitemia in this group was only 69%. A delivery cross-sectional survey at the same hospital found that two or more doses of IPTp with SP during pregnancy compared to none or one dose was not associated with any reduction in placental malaria for any gravidity (Gutman J. et al., 2013). However, two or more doses of IPTp with SP were found to reduce the prevalence of a composite birth outcome among primigravidae (i.e., any of the following: small for gestational age, prematurity, or low birth weight). The conclusion from this study is that two or more doses of IPTp with SP currently provides some small benefit to neonates but does not show the same effect seen in studies conducted when SP was more efficacious in treating *P. falciparum*. There is an urgent need for studies to evaluate other drugs that can be used as alternatives to SP in IPTp to reduce the effects of malaria in pregnancy.

Recent data from operational research in Malawi suggest that there is still a modest effect of SP when given as IPTp but recent studies from Tanzania and Malawi suggest that the presence of the sextuple mutation in the *P. falciparum* population can result in the failure of SP when given as IPTp. Currently, the presence of the sextuple mutant in Malawi is less than 10%. Given the effect of these mutations on the efficacy and safety of IPTp with SP, PMI will support monitoring of key *P. falciparum* resistance markers among pregnant women at ANC to identify increases in the prevalence and distribution of the sextuple mutant (see Monitoring and Evaluation section for further detail).

Additionally, PMI will support a delivery cross-sectional survey to monitor the effectiveness of IPTp with SP. The survey will be conducted in three locations in Malawi and will provide information on whether IPTp-SP continues to reduce placental parasitemia and intrauterine growth retardation despite high levels of SP resistance among malaria parasites in Malawi. The survey is a follow-up to the original IPT-Mon study in 2011 (see Monitoring and Evaluation section for further detail).

Gap analysis

The number of pregnant women in Malawi in 2015 is estimated to be 815,522 (5% of the population). To ensure that each pregnant woman receives three doses of SP, approximately 2.4 million SP treatments will be needed in 2015.

Planned activities with FY 2014 funding and justification

The plan for activities to reduce malaria in pregnancy is to continue to support the procurement of SP and the promotion of health education messages at national and community levels to improve IPTp coverage. In addition, PMI will continue to provide free LLINs for routine distribution at ANC visits (see LLIN section). PMI will procure ANC supplies to ensure directly observed therapy and improved IPTp uptake at ANCs. PMI will provide funding to support anticipated IPTp policy changes in line with potential revisions to WHO IPTp policy recommendations in 2015.

Description and budget for proposed activities ($740,000)

- Procurement and distribution of approximately 2.4 million treatment doses of quality-assured SP to provide up to three SP doses per pregnancy ($290,000);

- Procurement of ANC supplies (cups and water buckets) to improve IPTp uptake ($50,000);

- Support for strengthening focused antenatal care programs nationwide through joint trainings with the RHU on IPTp and proper implementation of the new IPTp guidelines as well as quarterly, joint supervision visits and mentoring health providers ($300,000);

- Support monitoring of key *P. falciparum* resistance markers among pregnant women at ANC clinics to identify increases in the prevalence and distribution of the sextuple mutant, which is associated with the failure of IPTp with SP. This monitoring will provide the information needed for Malawi to react to new recommendations for IPTp that may be forthcoming (funding listed in M&E section);

- Support for evaluation of SP resistance levels to inform IPTp policy (funding listed in M&E section).

- Support to changes in IPTp policy in 2015 in line with anticipated revised WHO recommendations on new medicines. Support will be for developing the new policy guidelines, dissemination, and training ($100,000).

4. Case Management

Diagnostics

NMCP/PMI objectives

Increasing malaria diagnostic capacity to ensure prompt and effective disease management and reduce the unnecessary use of antimalarial medications is a key priority in Malawi's 2011-2015 Malaria Strategic Plan. To achieve this increased capacity, the MoH is focusing its efforts in two main areas: 1) expanding the scope and improving the quality of microscopy services and 2) rolling out RDTs to all health facilities and village health clinics.

A revised version of the *Guidelines for the Treatment of Malaria in Malawi* was approved in late 2013. In this guide, the MoH recommends that all suspected malaria cases should be tested using an RDT prior to initiating treatment. Microscopy is recommended for the following purposes: to confirm malaria diagnosis in inpatients with suspected severe malaria; to monitor treatment progress in severe malaria cases receiving parenteral treatment; and to confirm first-line treatment failures.

Progress in the last 12 months

PMI continued to support the strengthening of diagnostic services through the outreach training and support supervision program. This program is designed to provide long-term, ongoing support and on-site training to strengthen diagnostic services in health facilities, including both microscopy and the appropriate use of RDTs. During scheduled visits, supervisors identify areas for improvement and provide immediate support to laboratory and clinical staff through on-site training. To maximize resources and minimize duplication of effort, malaria supervision is integrated with supervision and laboratory strengthening efforts for tuberculosis and PEPFAR.

Malawi has supervisory teams in each of its 29 districts and one national supervisory team supporting the outreach training and supportive supervision program. To date, these teams have provided supervisory support for 182 of the 190 health facilities with a laboratory. With FY 2012, FY 2013 and FY 2014 funding, further rounds of outreach training and supportive supervision will be undertaken with the goal of achieving and maintaining 100% coverage of health facilities with a laboratory. In addition to this program, PMI has also supported malaria diagnostic refresher training for 20 laboratory technicians to maintain the current technical capacity for malaria diagnosis.

The MoH has adopted a phased approach for the roll-out of malaria RDTs. Phase one, which is now complete, focused on the distribution and use of malaria RDTs at all health facilities, including those operated by the Christian Health Association of Malawi. Phase two, which is in the initial stages, will focus on the roll-out of RDTs for use at the community level using lessons learned from the health facility phase. A pilot study is currently underway to assess the feasibility, acceptability, and logistics of RDT use at this level of care and, when completed, it will further inform the roll-out to the community level, which is expected to commence toward the end of calendar year 2013. Thus far, PMI has supported the scale-up of RDT use through provision of technical support for policy and guideline revision, the procurement of RDTs, the training of health workers, and the promotion of appropriate malaria care and treatment among community members.

During the initial stages of the RDT roll-out to health facilities, commodity stockouts created problems and delays. However, additional procurements by the Global Fund and PMI (using FY 2011 and FY 2012 funds), combined with improved coordination of commodity deliveries, have resulted in normalization of stock levels.

Challenges, opportunities, and threats

The main challenges to reaching the goal of universal diagnostic coverage continue to be inadequate diagnostic technical capacity, including human resources, and shortages of diagnostic supplies at health facilities and VHCs. Currently, only 28% of health facilities have the capacity to provide malaria microscopy by trained and qualified laboratory staff. Expansion of microscopy services to additional facilities is limited by the lack of trained health workers, inconsistent electrical supply, and inadequate laboratory equipment and supplies. Even within facilities with trained and qualified staff, power supply interruptions and supply stockouts constrain microscope use.

The recent roll-out of RDTs to all health facilities has expanded diagnostic capacity, particularly for facilities that lack the capacity to perform malaria microscopy. Overall, this has reduced the reliance on presumptive diagnosis and moved Malawi closer to universal diagnostic coverage. Nevertheless, it will be important for the NMCP to maintain the capacity for microscopy in larger health facilities and hospitals to aid in the diagnosis and monitoring of severe malaria cases.

Although RDTs are now in use at the health facility level, the roll-out to the community level is yet to commence. This roll-out presents a significant opportunity and is critical to achieving the goal of universal diagnostic coverage. However, this phase will also present challenges related to commodity distribution, training, supportive supervision, and monitoring, which will need to be addressed.

Commodity gap analysis

To date, RDTs have been procured primarily with support from PMI and the Global Fund consolidated Rounds Two and Seven grant, which will end at the end of December 2013. At this time, no further funding for RDT procurement is planned under the Global Fund Round Nine Phase Two grant. However, even without future Global Fund support, carryovers from the significant procurements planned by the Global Fund and PMI in 2013 and 2014 will limit the projected gap for 2015 to approximately 3.3 million RDTs. The table below illustrates the projected RDT needs according to the NMCP's most recent quantification forecast, as well as and expected procurements through 2015.

Table 4. Projected RDT Needs and Expected Procurements

Calendar Year	2012	2013	2014	2015
Estimated RDT needs				
Estimated clinical malaria cases*	9,532,444	9,808,885	10,093,343	10,386,049
Reduction in RDT needs after accounting for RDT coverage†	3,431,680	3,138,843	1,917,735	519,302
Total estimated RDT needs	**6,100,764**	**6,670,042**	**8,175,607**	**9,866,747**
RDT resources				
Global Fund‡	398,875	0	5,650,850	0
PMI	3,365,525	9,225,575	4,000,000	3,300,000
GOM	2,500,000	0	0	0
Total RDT resources	**6,264,400**	**9,225,575**	**9,650,850**	**3,300,000**
Carry over	**614,731**	**778,367**	**3,333,900**	**4,809,143**
Surplus (Gap)	**778,367**	**3,333,900**	**4,809,143**	**(1,757,605)**

* Estimated based on a combination of consumption and morbidity data.
† Assumptions: 80% of patients visit health facilities and 20% visit CCM, completion of RDT roll-out to health facilities in 2012 and to CCM in 2015, and a progressive increase in RDT coverage (i.e. 80% in 2012, 85% in 2013, 90% in 2014 and 95% in 2015)
‡ Assumes a reduction of 708,100 RDTs in 2014 from the originally proposed Global Fund Round 7 procurement. However, the final amount to be provided by Global Fund in 2014 is still to be determined.

Planned activities with FY 2014 funding and justification

With FY 2014 funds, PMI will continue to focus its support in three areas: 1) maintaining diagnostic quality improvement; 2) procuring RDTs and ancillary supplies; and 3) training and supportive supervision of health workers.

Description and budget for proposed activities ($3,200,000)

- Strengthen microscopy and RDT use as part of larger laboratory strengthening effort including the expansion of supportive supervision to CHAM facilities. In addition, PMI will support efforts to expand the community case management program (see Treatment: Challenges, opportunities, and threats section below) and provide training and supervision for HSAs on RDT use in districts not currently covered ($1,000,000);

- Procurement and distribution of 3.3.million RDTs ($2,050,000);

- Procurement and distribution of ancillary diagnostic supplies, specifically gloves and sharps containers ($150,000);

- Provide technical assistance and support for strengthening malaria case management at the health facility and community level through an integrated health systems strengthening program that includes malaria in pregnancy, diagnostic, and treatment components. Diagnostic-specific activities will focus on continued support for the phased RDT implementation, including training and supervision on the correct and consistent use of RDTs in the evaluation of patients with fever (funding included in the Treatment section).

Treatment

NMCP/PMI objectives

Malawi's 2011-2015 Malaria Strategic Plan calls for increased access to prompt and effective antimalarial treatment for all suspected and confirmed malaria cases. To achieve this goal, the MoH is prioritizing: 1) the training and supervision of health workers on malaria case management at all levels of the health system; and 2) the roll-out and support of community case management in hard-to-reach areas.

The revised *Guidelines for the Treatment of Malaria in Malawi*, which were finalized in late 2013, present the most up-to-date treatment guidance. For the management of uncomplicated malaria, AL remains the first-line treatment and ASAQ the second-line treatment. Oral quinine plus clindamycin is recommended for the treatment of uncomplicated malaria in pregnant women in the first trimester and for children weighing less than five kilograms. For the management of patients with severe malaria, parenteral artesunate is recommended as the definitive treatment. At health centers, intramuscular artesunate is recommended for pre-referral treatment for severe malaria, followed by prompt referral to a hospital for further evaluation and management. Parenteral quinine may be used when parenteral artesunate is contraindicated or unavailable at the hospital or health center level. At the community level, the NMCP recommends prompt initiation of pre-referral therapy with rectal artesunate and immediate referral. (It should be noted that, at the time that this MOP was prepared, the roll-out for parenteral and rectal artesunate has not yet begun and these commodities are not yet available within the health system.)

Progress in the last 12 months

PMI continued to support the strengthening of malaria case management at the health facility and community levels and expanded the number of districts receiving PMI support from 12 to 15. At the facility level, PMI-supported activities focused on training and monitoring health workers in malaria case management as part of the integrated management of childhood illness package, as well as monitoring for the consistent availability of antimalarial commodities.

At the community level, PMI supported community case management implementation by equipping village health clinics and providing training, supervision, and monitoring to HSAs in the 15 PMI-supported districts. Of the 1,566 VHCs located in the 15 target districts, PMI currently provides support to 1,124 (72%). In addition, PMI supported community mobilization activities in the targeted districts to increase malaria prevention and care-seeking behaviors by community members.

PMI also provided technical and logistical assistance to the NMCP for the revision of case management policies and guidelines, including the *Guidelines for the Treatment of Malaria in Malawi,* the *Malaria in Pregnancy Guidelines for Health Workers in Malawi,* and the health worker training manuals associated with the guidelines.

Artemether-lumefantrine was provided with support from both PMI and the Global Fund consolidated Rounds Two and Seven grants. PMI worked closely with the NMCP and the Global Fund to coordinate procurement and delivery schedules to ensure that appropriate central stock levels of AL were maintained. PMI also procured 485,000 ampules of parenteral artesunate using FY 2012 funds to support the introduction this commodity, planned for the latter part of 2013.

As in past years, PMI continued to fund quarterly end-use verification surveys to assess the supplies and usage of malaria-related commodities at a sample of health facilities. These survey results are nationally representative when aggregated annually.

Challenges, opportunities, and threats

Malawi has made steady progress toward ensuring effective case management at the health facility and community level; however, several challenges remain. First, although the implementation of a parallel supply chain system for malaria commodities has significantly reduced the frequency of stockouts, inconsistent supplies of antimalarial medications at the facility and community level still limit the ability of health workers to appropriately treat malaria patients (see Pharmaceutical and Supply Chain Management section below). Overconsumption, particularly of AL, continues to complicate efforts to project the quantities needed annually.

Second, a significant portion of PMI support for case management activities is channeled through an integrated service delivery platform that is targeted to 15 of the 29 districts in Malawi. Although PMI has supported nationwide case management activities through a separate implementing partner, the focus of these activities has been on the strengthening of diagnostic capacity. This has left a gap in support for other case management activities (e.g., training and supervision for community case management) that has been filled only partially by other development partners and agencies. Beginning in FY 2012, this diagnostic implementing partner has transitioned and the new implementing partner has an expanded scope. This provides an opportunity to extend PMI support for community case management to previously under-supported districts, allowing for greater access to appropriate case management for people living in rural, hard-to-reach areas and creating a stronger platform for the upcoming roll-out of pre-referral rectal artesunate.

Finally, with the planned introduction of rectal artesunate at the community level, concerns exist that referrals may not be completed following suppository administration, particularly if the patient's clinical status improves. In addition to training of HSAs on the importance of referral initiation and completion, sensitization of the community will be needed to ensure the appropriate management of severe malaria at this level.

Commodity gap analysis

Artemether-lumefantrine is primarily procured with support from the Global Fund and PMI. The following table presents the estimated AL needs and resources through 2015, as projected by the NMCP, including the proposed PMI contribution with FY 2014 funding. Notably, AL categorized as carry over represents funding for the equivalent amount of AL that was not purchased during the given year but will be used the following year. The carry over in 2012 and 2013 is higher than normal in anticipation of a projected AL shortfall due to the end of the Global Fund consolidated Rounds Two and Seven grant in December 2013. The carry over is projected to return to normal by 2015.

Table 6. Estimated AL Needs and Planned Procurements

Calendar Year	2012	2013	2014	2015
Estimated AL need				
Estimated malaria cases*	9,532,444	9,808,885	10,093,343	10,386,049
Reduction in cases requiring treatment due to negative parasitologic diagnosis†	1,982,748	2,334,515	3,065,853	3,946,699
Total estimated AL need	**7,549,696**	**7,474,370**	**7,027,490**	**6,439,350**
AL resources				
Global Fund‡	5,905,440	0	2,480,280	2,000,000
PMI	4,495,170	4,584,450	4,200,000	2,050,000
Total AL resources	**10,400,610**	**4,584,450**	**6,680,280**	**4,050,000**
Carry over	**2,787,096**	**5,638,010**	**2,748,090**	**2,400,880**
Surplus (Gap)	**5,638,010**	**2,748,090**	**2,400,880**	**11,529**

* Based on a combination of consumption and morbidity data
† Assumptions: 80% of patients visit health facilities and 20% visit CCM, completion of RDT roll-out to health facilities in 2012 and to CCM in 2015, progressive increase in RDT coverage (i.e. 80% in 2012, 85% in 2013, 90% in 2014 and 95% in 2015), a 50% test negativity rate, a progressive increase in compliance with RDT results (i.e. 65% in 2012, 70% in 2013, 75% in 2014 and 80% in 2015).
‡Assumes a reduction of 2,029,320 treatment courses in 2014 from the originally proposed Global Fund Round 7 procurement. However, the final amount to be provided in 2014 by Global Fund is still to be determined.

The MoH/NMCP estimate for the annual need for parenteral artesunate assumes that 200,000 cases of severe malaria will occur each year (i.e., 4.9 million cases of malaria, four percent of which are severe) and that 75% of these cases will occur in children less than five years of age. Approximately 75% these cases will receive one dose of pre-referral treatment at a peripheral health facility and all cases will receive four doses for definitive treatment.

PMI has initiated the procurement of 485,000 ampules of parenteral artesunate using FY 2012 funds and has plans to procure and distribute an additional 340,000 ampules using FY 2013 funds. As the table below illustrates, the MoH intends to cover the remaining need through the middle of 2016 with support from the Global Fund interim funding and UNITAID/Medicines for Malaria Venture.

Table 7. Estimated Parenteral Artesunate (Ampules) Needs and Planned Procurements

	MoH FY 2013*	MoH FY 2014*	MoH FY 2015*
Parenteral artesunate (ampules) need	**749,461**	**1,496,250**	**1,496,250**
Parenteral artesunate resources/supplies			
Global Fund	961	756,250	786,250
PMI	485,500	340,000	0
UNITAID (MMV)	100,000	400,000	710,000
Government of Malawi	163,000		
TOTAL	**749,461**	**1,496,250**	**1,496,250**
Surplus (Gap)	0	0	0

*The MoH fiscal year covers the period of July 1 – June 30

Although not presented here, the MoH also plans to cover the entire projected need for the second-line ACT (ASAQ) and rectal artesunate through MoH Fiscal Year 2015 with support from the Global Fund New Funding Model interim-funding grant. As a result, PMI does not intend to procure parenteral or rectal artesunate or ASAQ using FY 2014 funds.

Planned activities with FY 2014 funding and justification

PMI remains committed to supporting MoH efforts to provide prompt and effective malaria treatment. With FY 2014 funds, PMI proposes to procure approximately 30% of the estimated AL need for 2015. This contribution will cover the entire gap that remains after taking into consideration projected Global Fund procurements. PMI will also continue efforts to strengthen malaria case management at the facility and community levels through training and supportive supervision, including the expansion of support for community case management. Additional funding will also be targeted to BCC interventions focused on the appropriate management of severe malaria at the community level and support for supply system management and strengthening to ensure adequate and consistent supplies of antimalarials at the point of care.

Description and budget for proposed activities ($2,950,000)

- Procurement and distribution of approximately 2,050,000 AL treatment courses ($2,500,000);

- Provide continued technical assistance and support for strengthening malaria case management at the health facility and community levels through an integrated health system strengthening program that includes MIP, diagnostic, and treatment components. Treatment-specific activities will include: training and supervision to ensure appropriate patient assessment and management; support for community case management activities; and support for the implementation of rectal artesunate at the community level ($450,000);

- Support the expansion of community case management training and supportive supervision to districts not currently covered under the integrated health systems strengthening program (funding included in the Diagnostics section);

- Promote the initiation and completion of pre-referral assessment and treatment for severe malaria at the community level through an integrated community case management BCC campaign (funding included in Behavioral Change and Communication section);

- Provide continued support for the management of the PMI-Global Fund supply chain system for PMI procured commodities and technical assistance to the Government of Malawi to support efforts to reform the national supply chain management system (funding included in the Pharmaceutical and Supply Chain Management Section).

Pharmaceutical and supply chain management

NMCP/PMI objectives

The 2011-2015 Malaria Strategic Plan calls for a reliable, secure, and accountable pharmaceutical and supply chain management system to ensure the availability of essential commodities and supplies for malaria control and prevention activities. To achieve this objective, the NMCP plans to conduct annual forecasting and quantification, strengthen the logistics management information systems in collaboration with Health Technical Support Services (a directorate of the MOH and CMS), develop annual procurement plans in collaboration with partners, and support national and international efforts to strengthen the procurement and supply chain system.

Progress since the launch of PMI

Supply chain issues have been a key concern in Malawi. Due to issues of leakage and general mismanagement, a PMI-Global Fund supply chain was created in late 2010 to distribute all USG and Global Fund supported commodities. In mid-2011, CMS reached the point of near-collapse when its procurement systems became de-capitalized due to continued non-payment of arrears by district governments. In response, the GoM submitted an emergency request for procurement support from health donors, which resulted in the creation of an 18-month multi-donor emergency essential drugs project. The purpose of the project was to immediately improve the availability of essential medicines and support CMS reform by temporarily lightening the burden on CMS systems and contributing to its recapitalization with GoM funds freed up from the district level.

Efforts to reform CMS have continued since 2011. The CMS was established as an independent public trust with a Board of Trustees and the Board appointed a new Chief Executive Officer. Significant infrastructure upgrades have been undertaken to improve warehousing through joint funding between the Global Fund and the GoM, and plans are underway to transfer storage of HIV commodities to CMS. Additional reforms include new staffing policies, a newly developed business plan, improved coordination with districts and the PMI-Global Fund supply chain, implementation of the recapitalization plan and prevention of districts from continuing to amass debt, and development of plans to facilitate the transition of the essential drug program to CMS in September 2013.

In addition to support for CMS reform, the USG has supported efforts to improve the overall supply chain through continued support to the MoH – to both the pharmaceutical services department (Health Technical Support Services) and the NMCP – to strengthen planning and coordination centrally and improve commodity management and reporting at the district and facility levels. Support to the central level has included technical assistance to implement annual national quantification and forecasting of all essential medicines, conduct supply planning and monitoring for malaria commodities, support Supply Chain Manager and the National Stock Status Database, and support planning and supervision by the NMCP. Support to the district, health center, and community levels has included quarterly supervision and end-use verification surveys, ongoing support to operate and expand access to Supply Chain Manager for the LMIS, and support to improve access to malaria commodities for community-level distribution through CCM. To help improve commodity management at the facility level and overcome critical human resources shortages, the MoH plans to recruit and place a new cadre of pharmacy assistants to manage commodities. In the interim, the USG has supported a MoH initiative to train two HSAs per health center and HSA supervisors on stock management to improve inventory management and LMIS reporting.

Progress in the last 12 months

The NMCP and PMI continue to focus on minimizing or eliminating stockouts of malaria commodities at service delivery points and strengthening supply planning and commodity management through planning, training and supportive supervision. Activities conducted in 2012 include monthly commodity distributions, quarterly end-use verification surveys, integrative supportive supervision, LMIS reporting, and capacity building. Since June 2012, the percentage of facilities reporting stockouts has been less than ten percent each month. Two rounds of field visits for end-use verification surveys and for integrative supportive supervision were done in collaboration with the NMCP and Health Technical Support Services, respectively. Capacity building activities included refresher courses for approximately 1,100 HSAs trained as drug store clerks and 410 in-charge supervisors. Additionally, approximately 2,500 dispensing registers were produced and distributed to all health facilities.

In August 2012, representatives from the GoM, CMS, and several partners, including WHO, the Global Fund, DfID, and PMI, conducted a review of the supply chain management system and developed a *Joint Strategy for Supply Chain Integration in Malawi*. To provide a roadmap for CMS reform, the planning team conducted site visits to all CMS facilities and selected health facilities; held broad consultations with government, private sector, and development partners; and conducted a series of in-depth, joint planning sessions. The roadmap included four distinct phases of integration in which the CMS will gradually take on additional supply chain functions currently managed by the PMI-Global Fund supply chain. The four phases include CMS recapitalization and reform, management of essential drugs supply chain, integration of additional PMI-Global Fund supply chain warehousing and distribution, and integration of procurement functions. Decision-making at each phase will be informed by ad hoc external assessments and a mid-term review of CMS's capabilities as measured by 36 specific benchmarks, representing specific standards of performance that CMS will be expected to meet at each phase as pre-conditions for integration. Decisions will be undertaken collaboratively between the CMS, MOH and development partners and will be subject to specific development partner requirements regarding the commodities in question. Although timeframes were not specified in the strategy, implementation of the first three phases are likely to extend beyond 2013 based on the rapid assessment of the current CMS functioning conducted during the August 2012 joint mission.

Challenges, opportunities, and threats

Existing issues such as lack of human resources for commodity management and limited knowledge on stock management, ordering, and planning continue to hinder the system. In addition to donor support for CMS reform, the GoM Department of Treasury has committed 1 billion Malawi Kwacha (approximately $3,500,000) annually to pay down the district debt to CMS. Nevertheless, the CMS continues to face an uphill battle to re-establish its credibility and regain the trust of clients (districts and health facilities) as well as the donor community. The *Joint Strategy for Supply Chain Integration* provides strong direction and guidance in this regard.

Without increased investment in core capacities of the national supply system, even a fully successful CMS reform process and full reintegration of the PMI-Global Fund supply chain will not be able to address stockouts and ensure a reliable supply of malaria commodities to the end user.

PMI supports two technical assistants, who are seconded to the Health Technical Support Services. The presence of these advisors provides an opportunity to improve the MoH capacity to coordinate pharmaceuticals and supply chain management in Malawi.

Planned activities with FY 2014 funding and justification

PMI remains committed to supporting the operation of the PMI-Global Fund supply chain and MoH efforts to strengthen commodity management and planning at all levels of the system. PMI and the USG will need to continue to monitor and support the ongoing CMS reform and transition to determine when to reenter the CMS system.

Description and budget for proposed activities ($1,800,000)

- Provide support for receipt, warehousing, management and oversight, and physical distribution of PMI-procured case management commodities through the PMI-Global Fund supply chain management system directly to the health facility level ($1,100,000);

- Provide support for technical assistance for MoH pharmaceutical and supply chain management activities including building leadership and human capacity for supply chain management, strengthening district supply chains, supporting efforts to reform LMIS, enabling appropriate oversight and quality assurance, and ensuring strong coordination between key stakeholders ($700,000).

5. Monitoring and Evaluation, Surveillance, and Operations Research

NMCP/PMI objectives

The 2011-2015 Malaria Strategic Plan calls for strengthening of surveillance, monitoring and evaluation systems through routine health management information systems, malaria-specific surveillance and special surveys to gather entomologic, epidemiologic, and coverage indicator data. The Malaria Strategic Plan also includes objectives related to operational research through the support of local capacity building. The 2011-2015 National Malaria Monitoring and Evaluation Plan was finalized in the first quarter of 2012. This plan follows the principles of the Roll Back Malaria (RBM) monitoring and evaluation guidance to provide a comprehensive framework for obtaining reliable and consistent data to assess progress toward the achievement of universal coverage of malaria interventions and the reduction of disease burden.

Progress since the launch of PMI

National household surveys

The MICS completed in 2006 by UNICEF provides the baseline data for PMI's program. Although it provided information on net ownership and usage, as well as IPTp uptake, it did not include any biomarker data. The NMCP, with assistance from the Malaria Control and Evaluation Partnership in Africa, completed Malawi's first Malaria Indicator Survey in April 2010. The results documented increases in household net ownership, net usage in vulnerable groups, and uptake of IPTp. Nevertheless, high parasitemia (~43%) was noted. PMI provided support to the 2010 Demographic and Health Survey, which provided district-level estimates of under-five mortality and malaria indicators.

Other surveys

Health facility surveys

In 2011, PMI supported a nationwide health facility survey to assess the quality of malaria case management in outpatient facilities. Results from this evaluation showed that nearly one-third of patients with uncomplicated malaria confirmed by microscopy were not appropriately treated for malaria, primarily due to missed diagnoses. This survey preceded the roll-out of RDTs and it is hoped that the expansion of malaria diagnostic services will lead to improved case management practices.

End-use verification surveys

PMI began supporting end-use verification surveys with FY 2011 funds. Initial surveys identified high percentages of facilities reporting stockouts – 38%-55% of facilities with stockouts of three or more days across each AL presentation and approximately 75% of facilities with stockouts of SP. Reporting through the logistics management information system has been incomplete and inconsistent. As a result, the end-use verification surveys have been an essential tool to help guide and improve inventory management of commodities at the health facility level.

Antimalarial therapeutic efficacy testing

Malawi has continued to monitor the efficacy of its first- (artemether-lumefantrine) and second-line (artesunate-amodiaquine) antimalarial drugs through *in-vivo* drug efficacy studies conducted every two years. PMI supported studies in one location (Machinga District Hospital) with FY 2010 funding that included the first- and second-line therapies plus dihydroartemisinin piperaquine, a potential future drug for Malawi. A second efficacy study has been funded with FY 2013 funding and is due to start in 2014. The results of the first study, which are pending at the time of writing (see Progress in the last 12 months), will help to guide PMI and Malawi's decision-making regarding prompt and effective case management of malaria including the possibility of alternate drug regimens.

Malaria surveillance and routine systems

Health facility surveillance

PMI initially supported health facility surveillance via sentinel sites in Malawi from FY 2007 through FY 2010. However, PMI discontinued support for sentinel sites in FY 2011 based on an evaluation that found a key indicator for data quality – the proportion of suspect malaria cases that were laboratory confirmed - continued to remain low.

The primary system for monitoring the implementation of services for the Ministry of Health in Malawi is the Health Management Information System. The HMIS collects and reports data on 74 core indicators, including outpatient suspected malaria cases and inpatient malaria deaths. However, reporting has been incomplete and inconsistent and has often lacked parasitologic confirmation. In an attempt to improve system performance, the HMIS began to transition the information system from DHIS to DHIS 2 in 2009. The DHIS 2 is a web-based system for capturing data at district level but maintains paper-based reporting at health facility level. The DHIS 2 also allows for capture of additional of malaria-specific indicator variables. While the MoH has been overhauling the HMIS, the NMCP was granted authority to develop a parallel reporting system for malaria surveillance in 2011. PMI supported this activity through training of district health management teams in the parallel system surveillance forms and mentoring visits from the NMCP monitoring and evaluation (M&E) officers.

Since 2010, PMI has seconded an M&E officer to the NMCP. The M&E officer has played a key role in building M&E capacity within the NMCP by supporting routine malaria surveillance, assisting in planning and analysis of national population-based surveys in conjunction with the National Statistics Office, and institutionalizing M&E systems to track the status of key malaria indicators. Starting in FY 2013, this M&E officer will be supported for a two year period using USG Global Fund technical assistance funding.

Table 8. Monitoring and Evaluation Activity Summary Table

	2006	2007	2008	2009	2010	2011	2012	2013	2014	2015
Household surveys	MICS*				DHS† MIS§		MIS¶		MIS	DHS
Other surveys	Subnational A&P survey	Subnational A&P survey	Subnational A&P survey	Evaluation of c-IMCI program		Health facility survey: malaria case mgmt. in outpatient facilities	Health facility survey: Mgmt. of severe malaria in inpatient facilities			
						EUV	EUV/ SPA**	EUV	EUV	
						TES			TES	
Malaria surveillance and routine systems		Entomological monitoring	Entomological monitoring	Entomological monitoring	Entomological monitoring	Entomological monitoring	Entomological monitoring	Entomological monitoring	Entomological monitoring	
		Sentinel site surveillance	Sentinel site surveillance	Sentinel site surveillance	Sentinel site surveillance	Routine health information system	Routine health information system	Routine health information system	Routine health information system	
									Electronic medical records system ††	

* MICS conducted by UNICEF, report available at
http://www.childinfo.org/files/MICS3_Malawi_FinalReport_2006_eng.pdf

† DHS available at http://www.measuredhs.com/what-we-do/survey/survey-display-333.cfm

§ MIS conducted with technical assistance from the Malaria Control and Evaluation Partnership in Africa (MACEPA), report available at http://www.givewell.org/files/DWDA%202009/AMF/Malawi_MIS_2010_Final.pdf

¶ MIS conducted by ICF-MACRO, data and report available at http://www.measuredhs.com/what-we-do/survey/survey-display-432.cfm

** SPA conducted in the last quarter of 2012 and first half of 2013

†† One-time support to develop and incorporate malaria-specific indicators into an electronic medical records data management system.

Operational research

PMI-funded operational research has supported systematic data collection activities that provide important data for decision-making, including studies measuring the durability of long-lasting ITNs, the effectiveness of the IPTp strategy, and studies examining the effectiveness of ITNs in an area with significant pyrethroid resistance.

Progress in the last 12 months

National household surveys

With FY 2012 funding, PMI supported the second MIS in Malawi. With funding and support from PMI, Malawi and the RBM partnership completed an impact evaluation of malaria control efforts between 2000 and 2010. The *Progress and Impact Series* report was launched in April 2013. Key findings include a 41% reduction in under-five mortality from 188 to 112 deaths per 1000 live births over the period 1996-2000 and 2006-2010, and modeling, which estimated that approximately 21,600 deaths among children under five years of age were prevented by malaria control interventions.

Other surveys

Health facility surveys

With FY 2011 funding, PMI supported a nationally representative survey of the quality of severe malaria case management in 36 tertiary care facilities. More than 1,200 inpatient medical records were reviewed for inpatients with suspected malaria diagnoses and 200 healthcare workers were interviewed regarding knowledge of care guidelines. Results from this evaluation identified limited availability of medications and diagnostic supplies due to facility-level stockouts and knowledge gaps among health workers as some of the main obstacles to providing quality care to patients with severe malaria.

End-use verification surveys and service provision assessment

In collaboration with the NMCP, two rounds of end-use verification survey field visits were completed. There was a reduction in stockouts of three or more days across each AL presentation from the previous end-use verification survey (range between 15% - 30%) to the most recent end-use verification survey (range between 13% - 19%). Overstocking remains a problem in a substantial proportion of facilities (approximately 40% and 70% of facilities for AL and SP, respectively), but the situation is improving. The last two quarterly surveys were not carried out because a service provision assessment was being conducted during November 2012 – June 2013.

Antimalarial therapeutic efficacy testing

Results from the therapeutic efficacy study (TES) funded with FY 2010 funding are pending and should be available by the end of 2013. Delays in the trial were caused by the need to obtain trial insurance to receive regulatory approval for the use of dihydroartemisinin-piperaquine and by recruitment that was slower than expected.

Monitoring molecular markers to monitor effectiveness of IPTp-SP

Recent data from operational research in Malawi suggest that there is still a modest effect of SP when given as IPTp but recent studies from Tanzania and Malawi suggest that the presence of the sextuple mutation in the *P. falciparum* population can result in the failure of SP when given as IPTp. Currently, the presence of the sextuple mutant in Malawi is less than 10%. Given the effect of these mutations on the efficacy and safety of IPTp with SP, PMI will begin monitoring the prevalence of the sextuple mutation in Malawi in 2014. This monitoring will be designed to provide the NMCP with the information needed to determine when and how to implement alternative approaches for the prevention of malaria in pregnancy (if and when alternative approaches are recommended by WHO and the prevalence of the mutation in the population is found to have increased). Alternatively, if monitoring reveals that the levels of these mutations remain low, this information may provide some assurance that SP for IPTp is still effective at reducing the burden of malaria in pregnancy.

Effectiveness of ITNs in an area of intense pyrethroid resistance

ITNs are the primary malaria prevention strategy in Malawi, and increasing resistance of malaria vectors to the only class of insecticides, pyrethroids, approved for use on ITNs threatens the future of malaria control in the country. PMI and CDC funded a study of the effectiveness of ITNs in a part of the country, Machinga District, with high levels of pyrethroid resistance among *An. funestus* and *An. gambiae* s.l. The first year of the study concluded in mid-2013 and results will be available by the end of the calendar year. The second part of the study, continuing to monitor ITN effectiveness as they age, will conclude in December 2013.

Entomologic and insecticide resistance monitoring
The NMCP and PMI have been discussing the development of a new entomologic monitoring plan to capture the most important variation across vector species, ecologic and agricultural zones to monitor insecticide resistance in areas representative of the entire country. To date, sentinel sites have been located primarily in the seven districts where IRS activities have been conducted, however, PMI and the NMCP are reviewing the entomological monitoring strategy and will relocate some sites to better represent the distinct eco-epidemiological zones in Malawi.

Malaria surveillance

Health facility surveillance

With support from the PMI M&E headquarters team, the PMI Malawi team conducted an informal review of the existing routine health information systems, including the Integrated Disease Surveillance and Response (IDSR), HMIS, and electronic medical records systems. The informal review found notable progress in HMIS reforms, including the plan to use the electronic DHIS 2 information system for transmission of data from the district to central level. The electronic DHIS 2 information system was rolled out to the districts during the first half of 2012. Because the IDSR framework is targeted more towards epidemic diseases and rapid response, it was not thought to be the most appropriate platform for routine malaria data collection at this time, but it should be considered in the future as the incidence of malaria decreases and outbreak detection becomes more important.

Since the completion of this informal PMI review, the NMCP has made significant progress toward the re-integration of the parallel malaria data collection system with the HMIS. With support from PMI and other partners, the NMCP has worked with the Central Monitoring and Evaluation Department of the MoH to ensure that appropriate malaria indicators (including commodity indicators) have been included in the DHIS 2 malaria-specific platform. Additionally, the collection forms used at the health facility level have been revised to mirror the indicators in the DHIS 2 and the use of parallel system reporting forms is being eliminated. In the short to medium term, the NMCP plans to continue to improve data collection and analysis within the HMIS through increased training and oversight of data entry and analysis staff at the district and health facility levels, as well as ensuring the availability of reporting forms and other necessary materials.

PMI also supported intensive training and supervision in 15 districts to improve paper-based reporting at the health facility level. The objective was to improve data quality and reporting from the health facility to the district level so that quality data would be available once the electronic DHIS 2 was rolled out. Data quality assessment exercises are currently underway to assess the impact of this intervention.

Although in its infancy in Malawi, the use of electronic medical record systems holds promise for the future. The MoH is currently working with an NGO to design and implement the electronic medical records system to assist healthcare workers with registering patients and aggregating essential medical data for improved healthcare management. The electronic medical records system has been implemented in selected district hospitals and health facilities, primarily in the central region of Malawi. With one-time FY 2012 funding, PMI is supporting NMCP efforts to incorporate malaria specific data fields into the electronic medical records system, which would link patient records with laboratory results. Although this effort is currently limited in geographic scope and will not provide robust data in the near term, efforts to support the electronic medical records system should be viewed as a way to augment the central system in the near to mid-term, with potential longer-term benefits as it is scaled up.

Challenges, opportunities, and threats

Routine monitoring of malaria indicators remains a challenge. Nevertheless, progress toward improved data collection is being made at the health facility level while the DHIS 2 is being implemented from the central to district level. Continued support from PMI will be critical as the new system is implemented.

Planned activities with FY 2014 funding ($1,459,000)

PMI plans to continue to support strengthening of routine health management information systems and malaria-specific surveillance and special surveys to gather entomologic, epidemiologic, and coverage indicator data. Specifically, with FY 2014 funding, PMI will:

- Provide partial support for the planned 2015 DHS ($459,000);
- Continue to strengthen routine data collection through training and supervision of data collection at health facility level and implementation of DHIS 2 in highly malaria endemic districts ($200,000);
- Support quarterly end-use verification surveys to assess the availability of malaria commodities at health facilities ($100,000);
- Continue support for entomologic monitoring with routine surveys of vector density and insecticide resistance testing of mosquitoes collected from sentinel villages in at least three districts (up to a total maximum of seven districts) where the NMCP is conducting IRS ($350,000);
- Support monitoring of key *P. falciparum* resistance markers among pregnant women at ANC clinics to identify increases in the prevalence and distribution of the sextuple mutant, which is associated with the failure of IPTp with SP. This monitoring will provide the information needed for Malawi to react to new recommendations for IPTp that may be forthcoming ($75,000);
- Support a delivery cross-sectional survey to monitor the effectiveness of IPTp with SP. The survey will be conducted in three locations in Malawi and will provide information on whether IPTp-SP continues to reduce placental parasitemia and intrauterine growth retardation despite high levels of SP resistance among malaria parasites in Malawi. The survey is a follow-up to the original IPT-Mon study in 2011 ($275,000).

6. Behavior Change Communication

NMCP/PMI Objectives

The National Malaria Strategic Plan calls for strengthening advocacy, communication, and social mobilization capacities to move towards optimal coverage for all malaria interventions. As such, the 2011-2015 Malaria Communication Strategy promotes an integrated approach to behavior change communication using social mobilization and advocacy. Social mobilization emphasizes the role and responsibility of the community in the control of malaria and uptake of interventions while promoting community members' participation in local initiatives to improve malaria prevention and control behaviors. Another important aspect of BCC is targeting health providers to utilize effective case management and malaria in pregnancy strategies for improved health outcomes. Advocacy focused at the national level is essential to mobilize political commitment and resources for malaria prevention and control efforts.

Progress since the launch of PMI

Since PMI began work in Malawi in 2007, PMI has supported an integrated approach to BCC focusing on ITNs, MIP, and case management. BCC activities have centered on national campaigns to promote year-round universal ITN use, large-scale campaigns to emphasize ANC attendance for IPTp and other antenatal services, and community-based campaigns that emphasize ITN utilization as well as improved case management through the promotion of improved care-seeking behaviors. Behavior change communication strategies have been employed from the national to the community level and targeted policy makers, health care providers, and community members. In promoting these interventions, PMI has utilized a variety of BCC approaches, including educational meetings, mass media, print media, community drama, and interpersonal communication activities. The small grants program has remained a central component of the BCC strategy to ensure good coverage and reach of BCC activities in all districts where PMI's implementing partners work.

Results from the 2012 MIS suggest that BCC efforts have been effective in conveying information that led to appropriate health behavior. Approximately one-quarter of Malawian women reported having seen or heard messages about malaria in the six months prior to the survey. Of those women, 42% heard a message about the importance of sleeping under a net. In terms of behavioral practices, according to the 2012 MIS nearly 81% of children aged less than five years slept under an ITN the night before the survey in households where at least one ITN was available. Although the causal link and quantification of contribution is difficult to establish, it would be reasonable to assume that our efforts did make some contribution in promoting ITN use in households in Malawi.

Progress during the last 12 months

In FY 2012, PMI transitioned its BCC program to a new implementing partner that integrates messages within a larger program of BCC messages, including maternal and child health and

HIV. The objectives remain in line with the NMCP strategic plan focusing on building capacity of key national institutional partners, strengthening national and community level planning and coordination, developing and producing evidence-based social BCC packages under a multi-level media campaign, and identifying and implementing best practices.

Start-up for the new BCC partner was slow over the past 12 months, as they established themselves in-country and built a relationship with the NMCP to implement BCC activities that support the national communication strategy. The partner has undertaken a two-pronged approach to BCC by bringing together communications and health services components.

Communications teams consisting of HSAs and PMI implementing partner community extension workers collaborate with the communities to identify key health issues. The teams then provide solutions to address these issues in an effort to bring about appropriate behavior for improved health outcomes. At the household and village level, communications teams have also concentrated on interpersonal communication activities to promote early and frequent ANC attendance, appropriate and prompt health-seeking behaviors and LLIN use. Community mobilization to increase acceptance and uptake of integrated vector management activities have been completed as well.

In the past 12 months in PMI-program areas, six malaria-specific radio spots have aired over 1,900 times, 39 of 53 radio programs in the project districts have integrated malaria messages into their health programming, and a new national radio program has been designed. A partnership was formed with the United Against Malaria global campaign in which nationally-renowned sports icons deliver messages to promote malaria prevention behaviors especially in adolescent populations. Major progress was in capacity building through training of 74 Community Mobilization Trainers trained in 15 PMI-program districts, 25 national- and district-level staff in strategic health communication, and 6,906 CHWs and CHVs in malaria prevention in six districts. Public awareness and sensitization activities oriented 2,790 community leaders in malaria prevention and 389,543 individuals (over 75% female) were reached with malaria messages through IPC and community outreach in six districts. The monitoring and evaluation component of the BCC program has been less well developed. Most interim reports have been focused on documenting activities conducted. PMI planned for an independent assessment of BCC activities with FY 2012 funding, but the assessment did not take place since the malaria communication strategy was to be revised in 2013. This assessment will be postponed until ample time has elapsed for an informative assessment.

Challenges, opportunities, and threats

The challenge remains of meeting both PMI and NMCP targets for malaria prevention and control. The 2012 MIS shows that 32% of children under five who had fever two weeks prior to the survey, only half (50%) sought treatment and one-fifth (20%) had blood taken for testing. These figures are low compared to the target of 90% for early care seeking and universal diagnosis (100%). Here lies the opportunity to intensify community and health provider messaging to improve this intervention.

Uptake of IPTp 2 is still sub-optimal (MIS 2012 54% vs. target 85%). With the recent modifications of the GoM IPTp policy to increase IPTp to at least three doses, PMI plans to focus BCC messaging both at community and national levels for improved service provision and utilization of ANC services by pregnant women.

The GoM has also recently changed its policy for treatment of severe malaria cases at community level. Diagnoses with rapid diagnostic tests as well as the pre-referral treatment with rectal artesunate are new concepts at community level for case management. For optimal policy implementation, PMI BCC activities have been planned to bring about an understanding of acceptability and using that information to foster increased utilization and demand of the new interventions.

The BCC program has gathered momentum by building on the success of previous efforts and integration with other health education programs. In addition to an integrated approach, malaria-specific messaging is still a necessary piece of the communications package to focus on the unique aspects of malaria prevention. To facilitate malaria-specific messaging, the implementing partner hired a malaria specialist to work within the program.

Planned activities with FY 2014 funding and justification

PMI plans to continue support for an integrated BCC approach at the national and community level for ITN, IPTp, and case management specific messaging.

National level efforts will focus on advocacy, mass media communication, and materials development. The national level communications campaigns will use radio and other mass media channels to encourage universal ITN use, increase awareness of IPTp and demand for ANC services, promote universal diagnosis of suspected malaria cases and prompt evaluation of fever, and encourage compliance with treatment regimens.

Community level efforts will be coordinated through the small grants program, which will provide support to eligible Malawian-based NGOs to implement activities that increase uptake of the new IPTp policy of three or more doses of SP and to engage school-aged children in prevention activities. Specific activities will be determined by the NGOs, but may include community or social mobilization, training of community workers, radio listening clubs, and community theater. The NGOs will work together with the district health management teams to develop BCC-specific annual work plans. Monitoring to achieve maximum coverage and integration into District Implementation Plans will be a key component.

PMI will continue to focus efforts on school-aged children aged 5-14 years and adolescents, most of whom attend school, as they represent approximately one-third of the population in Malawi and are at risk for malaria (Malawi DHS 2010). In a recent survey of school-aged children in 50 schools in Zomba District, the parasitemia prevalence for children aged 5-14 years was 60%, while self-reported ITN use was below 40%, which is 30-50% lower than ITN usage rates reported in high-risk populations (MAC, unpublished data). With the upcoming LLIN mass distribution campaign, school-aged children are a prime group at whom to target BCC messages on ITN use. Additionally, more than 60% of females in Malawi begin childbearing prior to age 19 and primigravida are most susceptible to the effects of malaria in pregnancy (Malawi DHS 2010). Despite 60% coverage of pregnant women with two doses of IPTp in Malawi, the 2010 MIS showed considerably lower rates among adolescent mothers. School-aged females are an ideal group at whom to target antenatal care and MIP health messages.

In addition to the integrated BCC efforts, PMI plans to develop and pilot malaria-specific prevention messages and activities to support the initiation and completion of pre-referral rectal artesunate treatment for children under five years old.

Description and budget for proposed activities ($1,700,000)

- National level BCC will use both integrated and malaria-specific mass media campaigns to promote diagnosis and treatment of malaria, IPTp uptake, and ITN ownership and use for all household members. The mass media campaign on ITN ownership and use will intensify prior to the universal coverage campaign in 2015 ($700,000);

- In the 15 districts where PMI is active, malaria-specific communications campaigns will promote early care-seeking behavior, treatment adherence, and net care and repair. These communications campaigns will be implemented using interpersonal communication activities with local NGOs ($500,000);

- Improved IPTp uptake will be the focus of health facility level training to health care providers in the 15 SSDI districts. Community level activities, including folk theater, will be undertaken in all PMI program districts to create more awareness of and demand for ANC services ($100,000);

- Support NGOs in the Machinga District to engage school-aged children in malaria prevention activities. Communication channels for school-aged children will be school drama groups, folk theater, songs, school-based academic competitions, and sports-oriented games. Other target populations – including teachers, school supervisors, parent-teacher association members, out-of-school children and adolescents – will be reached through inter-personal communication methods. Frequency will vary by activity – some are monthly while others are weekly ($200,000);

- Targeted BCC activities to support the roll-out of pre-referral treatment for severe malaria in the 15 SSDI districts. Activities include health care provider training and community-level interpersonal communication for promotion of care seeking behavior and community awareness ($200,000);

- Integrated community case management BCC campaign to promote prompt evaluation of fever and encourage acceptance of ACTs and treatment compliance (funds included in case management section).

7. Health Systems Strengthening and NMCP Capacity Building

NMCP/PMI objectives

The 2011-2015 Malaria Strategic Plan calls for strengthening capacity in program management to achieve objectives at all levels of health service delivery by building human resource capacity, mobilizing and utilizing resources more effectively, providing policy direction and leadership, strengthening coordination, and strengthening procurement and supply chain management.

The NMCP plans to achieve these goals through strong leadership, creation of a supportive environment, improved infrastructure, equipment and supplies, and effective collaboration with partners. The number of NMCP staff has increased over the years, with focal persons identified and assigned for each intervention, which has enabled the program to provide more focused guidance for the implementation of the Malaria Strategic Plan.

One of the key principles of the GHI is building sustainability through health systems strengthening. Under the Malawi GHI strategy, efficient and synergistic improvements across the health sector will be targeted through efforts to train and retain health care workers; incentivize health workers to deliver higher quality services; build capacity of the Central Medical Stores to reliably supply health commodities; foster forecasting for rational use of drugs and improve quantity procurement; increase use of affordable and locally sustainable technologies; expand health information systems and link these systems across health programs; and provide broad-based support to the national laboratory system. The USG will also support the development of leadership and management systems at the ministry and district levels, including systems for human resources, monitoring and evaluation, and finance management.

USAID leverages and creates synergies with many other partners and private sector actors. USG agencies currently serve as chair on the Education and Agriculture Donor Groups and will chair the Health Donor Group in 2013-14. The GoM launched two new Presidential Initiatives, "Poverty and Hunger Reduction" and "Safe Motherhood" (which includes training nurses and other healthcare workers), demonstrating the GoM recognition of its fundamental development needs.

Progress in the last 12 months

The formulation and launch of the National Health Sector Strategic Plan 2011-2016 built upon the sustained gains made under the 2004-2010 Program of Work. Considerable improvements in the delivery of an Essential Health Package have been registered in reducing infant and child mortality rates, pneumonia case fatality and maternal mortality, and in maintaining high immunization coverage, among other areas. The launch of the 2011-2016 Health Sector Strategic Plan coincided with finalization of the Malawi Growth and Development Strategy, which is an overall development agenda for the GoM. The Health Sector Strategic Plan 2011-2016 will continue to focus on primary, secondary, and tertiary levels of health care delivery.

The MoH will strengthen its focus on policy and guideline development and evidence-based decision-making to improve overall effectiveness in health planning and management. The five MoH zones will continue to provide supervisory support to the districts and offer a link to the central level. To effectively monitor the performance of the health sector during the Health Sector Strategic Plan implementation period, the Health Systems Strengthening Framework, based on the principles of the Paris Declaration on Aid Effectiveness, will be utilized.

Impact Evaluation of Performance-Based Incentives pilot

USAID supported the GoM in designing and implementing a pilot project in performance-based incentives (PBI). The goal of the PBI pilot is to increase value for money in health by financing outputs. Specifically, PBI is designed to accelerate access to high quality essential health services; increase health worker motivation; and improve quality of care, thereby improving health outcomes. The intended beneficiaries are three District Health Management Teams and seventeen health facility teams in three pilot districts (population 1.3 million). The pilot will be implemented over a two year period. Afterward, a rigorous evaluation will determine the pilot's impact on equitable access to services, quality of care, provider motivation, and policy makers' perceptions, as well as assess the economic impact of the intervention package. The budget for the impact evaluation is $1.5 million over two years.

The impact evaluation will measure change in quality of care that is attributable to PBI. The evaluation will provide malaria-specific information on health outcomes – in terms of quality of care and improvements in case management, for example – in addition to information on other diseases.

Public Financial Management

The Public Financial Management reform program will improve the GoM's ability to budget, allocate, expend, track, and report on funding for key health programs, including malaria. After the reforms, the strengthened PFM will enhance donor confidence and help to unlock Global Fund grants – including malaria grants – as well as other donor resources – for implementation of the Health Sector Strategic Plan, which includes malaria prevention and control.

The budget for the Public Financial Management reform project is $40 million over 5 years. USAID's total contribution to the PFM is $9 million. Within the USAID Mission, PEPFAR, MCH, FP/RH, Sustainable Economic Growth, Education and DG are all contributing to the PFM. Outside of the Mission, donors to the PFM include: the World Bank, European Union, DfiD, Norway, GIZ, Irish Aid, DANIDA, ADB, and SIDA (Swedish). The contributions from

DfiD, Norway, and GIZ come from their contributions to the SWAp. Contributions will be managed through a Multi-Donor Trust Fund to be set up and administered by the World Bank.

Disbursements for the Public Financial Management reforms are performance driven. An annual review of the reform program will be conducted under the leadership of the World Bank. The review will be an independent evaluation of the achievements of the program against benchmarks established under the M&E framework, as well as targets set out in the previous year's annual work program. A yearly implementation plan and corresponding Multi-Donor Trust Fund disbursement will be based on the results of the annual report.

The Malawi Mission's support of the PFM reforms is linked directly to the desire of the Agency, Global Health Bureau, and the Mission team to implement Government to Government (G2G) funding in the health sector. G2G activities are vital to building a platform for long-term sustainability of the GoM and MoH capacities, including malaria control. The PFM is a foundational activity to enable the Mission to realize G2G funding. By contributing to the Multi-Donor Trust Fund, USAID leverages the resources of other donors for this critical health system reform.

Malawi Local Capacity Development

Malawi's public health system suffers from a severe shortage of human resources to deliver quality health services, including administering RDTs and ACTs. Although the population is over 15 million, the government health service has only eight pediatricians, 16 obstetricians and 2,500 nurses and midwives. Due to the severe human resources crisis in the country, many health tasks are shifted to health surveillance assistants (HSAs). HSAs are low-level health workers who are not properly trained in dispensing RDTs and ACTs (nor other important medicines), yet they are responsible for manning drug stores at health centers. Under the Malawi Local Capacity Development (MALOCAD) training program,[3] pharmacy technicians will be trained to replace the HSAs. MALOCAD's trained pharmacy technicians will provide much needed capacity at the health center to dispense and account for RDTs and ACTs.

PMI resources will be used to train the new pharmacy technicians entering the workforce. PMI funds from FY 2013 will be used for curriculum development and will leverage FY 2013 PEPFAR funding. PMI FY 2014 resources will be used to train 24 pharmacy technicians at the

---

[3] The Malawi Local Capacity Development program (MALOCAD) is a training program to strengthen the human resources capacity in the health sector. MALOCAD will support pre-service training of 500 eligible Malawians to study at Malawian tertiary institutions in the areas of maternal and child health, nursing, midwifery, pharmacy, laboratory, nutrition, family planning, and reproductive health. MALOCAD trainings will complement existing pre-service and in-service professional development activities supported by USAID/Malawi.

district level over a two-year period. Funds will support tuition, trainee materials, and room and board. Pharmacy technicians will be trained in logistics management systems, storing and dispensing drugs, conducting inventory, recording and reporting stock status, calculating orders, logistics monitoring, and supervision, among other activities. Upon completion of training, health workers are committed to work for the Ministry of Health for at least five years and will be placed in one of 57 health centers in three districts (Lilongwe Rural, Machinga, and Balaka) serving a population of over 2 million people.

MALOCAD fits within a broader, multi-donor initiative to strengthen Malawi's health system that is based on the Ministry of Health's four-year strategic plan for human resources for health (Human Resources for Health Strategic Plan 2012-2016). The HRH plan is aligned with the Health Sector Strategic Plan 2011-2016. Other donors to the initiative include the Global Fund, DfiD, Norway, UNFPA, CHAI, and the Gates Foundation. The GoM's contributions includes the subsidized training cost, salaries for post graduate participants, and established positions for newly qualified staff based on HRH strategy 2012-2016.

Challenges, opportunities, and threats
The human resources challenges in Malawi are acute and complex. Projections show that despite an investment of $53 million during the Emergency Human Resource Plan for Pre-Service Training Capacity, annual output of nurses increased by only 22%. Without a significant increase in output levels, current projections indicate it will take many years to achieve the basic number of health staff needed to provide minimum standards of service delivery in Malawi. The GoM estimates the pre-service training cost for the Health Sector Strategic Plan period 2011-2016 to be $20,555,000. The government has contributed $12,000,000.

The Health Sector Strategic Plan highlights numerous challenges faced by Malawi's health system including: 1) weak health commodities supply chain and logistics management system from the central to district level; 2) lack of significant investment in human resources for health for Malawi to achieve a fully-staffed health system; 3) poor infrastructure and lack of necessary equipment in health facilities; 4) inefficient program management; 5) poor quality data that negatively impacts the measurement of impact and outcomes; and 6) inefficient financial management systems at all levels. In light of these complex and interlinked challenges, the USG prioritized three health systems strengthening areas for greater support under the GHI: 1) human resources for health; 2) infrastructure; and 3) leadership, governance, management and accountability.

Within the Health Sector Strategic Plan, the GoM has prioritized the training of nurses as a key frontline cadre that will assist to deliver the Essential Health Package. The GoM priority infrastructure activities have been defined to encompass: 1) constructing and renovating fit-for-purpose, environmentally friendly physical spaces (health facilities, laboratories, and health care worker housing); 2) ensuring the required utilities are in place to provide constant water, electricity, sanitation, and other services; 3) designing useful, standardized spaces that streamline services and reduce the time burdens on both patients and providers; 4) expanding electronic data collection and other HMIS; and 5) providing basic furniture and equipment along with equipment maintenance and repair. The Health Sector Strategic Plan also highlights issues of leadership and management as key for improving effectiveness of implementation of health services. The GHI strategy is aligned to the Health Sector Strategic Plan and will continue to prioritize USG support to these efforts.

The NMCP continues to face funding and capacity challenges. The program lacks resources to facilitate basic coordination functions such as holding regular technical working group meetings, supporting forums to disseminate research, conducting planning with stakeholders, and undertaking short courses to maintain the knowledge base.

Planned activities with FY 2014 funding and justification

Working closely with other USG programs in Malawi, PMI will contribute to the GHI activities that support the Health Sector Strategic Plan's implementation and lie specifically under USG stewardship. Though PMI continues to address malaria-specific challenges, real and documented progress will require increased attention to strengthen the health system with in-country partners. PMI will work with other USG health programs to enhance infrastructure through small-scale improvements, such as providing internet routing to districts to assist with the transmission of electronic information (DHIS 2), improve health information systems through data quality audits, strengthen financial management and provide support to the NMCP to attend short courses and participate in regional and international meetings, including dissemination of best practices and research results. PMI will also work with the Peace Corps office in Malawi to identify two Peace Corps volunteers to work with the NMCP.

Description and budget for proposed activities ($1,410,000)

- PMI will provide support to the NMCP to hold technical working group and research dissemination meetings and support basic logistical and operational functioning, including printing, equipment maintenance, and internet time. This is a continuation of an activity that was funded with FY 2013 funds and the same level of funding is being maintained ($100,000);

- Support activities to build leadership and management skills for managers in the NMCP. Adopting an approach that offers off-site classroom/workshop training followed by an opportunity for coaching and mentoring support, the activity will meet the needs of frontline managers in senior positions who need appropriate management and leadership training and support. The activity will also target mid-level managers in leadership roles. The training will address the challenges in malaria program implementation in a decentralized services health system. The activity will yield improved accountability, greater collaboration, networking, and partnering for increased community participation. It is expected that many of the beneficiaries will be malaria program managers at central, zonal and district levels. Demonstrable health leadership outcomes by the NMCP will include: timely decision-making; improved accountability; enhanced use of evidence-based approaches in program development and resource allocation; and increased engagement of civil society ($30,000);

- PMI will also support the NMCP to participate in short courses, regional and international meetings to expand their knowledge base ($30,000);

- M&E strengthening activities will include supportive supervision and mentoring on data collection and reporting, refresher training on Data Quality Assurance and management, conducting Data Quality Audits, and support to implementation of the DHIS ($160,000);

- USAID and other donors will be supporting a study of the 2012 National Health Accounts. Major objectives of the NHA study are to quantify total expenditure on general health. PMI funds will focus specifically on malaria subaccounts. UNICEF and SWAp funds will support the general NHA. HIV expenditure analysis is conducted separately. PMI support will be used to document the flow of funds within the health system for malaria; describe the distribution of total expenditure on malaria; and evaluate the efficiency and equity in the allocation of resources among various functions and levels of care ($110,000);

- Support small scale infrastructure improvements with specific inputs to GHI Malawi's prioritized interventions, including ANC and labor and delivery settings that will be renovated with new approaches to maintenance developed to improve patient experiences, address referral deficiencies, enhance maternal and neonatal outcomes, and decrease loss-to-follow up. Specific activities will include renovating health facilities, ensuring that there are utilities in place such as electricity or solar panels and water, and provision of equipment. This activity is a continuation of support provided in FY 2013 with increased funding to reach more health facilities in the 15 SSDI districts ($100,000);

- In the 15 SSDI districts, internet routers will be installed to enable effective and timely transfer of electronic data/information to the national level. The activity builds upon existing electronic data systems in Malawi and will be carried out as part of a GHI cross-program effort funded proportionally from PMI, MCH, and other USAID health programs. This activity aims to improve data collection and reporting of malaria specific indicators from the district to the central level through existing health information systems. There is a particular focus on developing the synergy between lab and outpatient department registers to allow better tracking of confirmed malaria cases. Additionally, data collected also guides quantification and forecasting for malaria commodities, which helps maintain stock balances. Improving Internet access at the district level also allows for more effective implementation of the electronic DHIS 2 system. The MoH adopted this web-based integrated data platform to make facility and district level data available to program managers at all levels for decision-making. Facility and district level data for all programs are reported through this web-based platform ($100,000);

- Support the impact evaluation of the performance-based incentives pilot in three pilot districts (population 1.3 million). The pilot, implemented over a two-year period, will be evaluated to determine its impact on equitable access to services, quality of care, provider motivation, and policy makers' perceptions, as well as the economic impact of the intervention package. The evaluation will provide malaria-specific information on health outcomes – in terms of quality of care and improvements in case management, for example – in addition to information on other diseases ($250,000);

- Support for the Public Financial Management reforms will strengthen the GoM's ability to budget, allocate, expend, track, and report on funding for key health programs, including malaria. The PFM reform has a direct impact on Global Fund grant disbursements, as well as other donor funding. It is envisioned that the strengthened PFM will enhance donor confidence and unlock Global Fund money for malaria prevention and control. PMI Malawi requested $250,000 in FY 2013 funds to support the Public Financial Management (PFM) reforms and is requesting that this support be continued at the same level with FY 2014 funds. PMI's total contribution to the PFM will thus total $500,000. PMI contribution to the Mission-wide support for PFM in FY 2015 will depend on the outcomes achieved with FY 2013 and FY 2014 support ($250,000);

- Support for two Peace Corps volunteers to work with NMCP at the national level to strengthen the program according to identified needs and gaps. PMI will support two Peace Corps volunteers plus funding for small project activities ($30,000);

- Support for pre-service training of new pharmacy technicians entering the workforce. With FY 2014, PMI resources will be used to train 24 pharmacy technicians at the district level over a two-year period. Funds will support tuition, trainee materials, and room and board. Pharmacy technicians will be trained in logistics management systems, storing and dispensing drugs, conducting inventory, recording and reporting stock status, calculating orders, logistics monitoring, and supervision, among other activities. Upon completion of training, health workers are committed to work for the Ministry of Health for at least five years and will be placed in one of 57 health centers in three districts (Lilongwe Rural, Machinga and Balaka) serving a population of over 2 million people ($250,000).

8. Staffing and Administration

Two health professionals serve as Resident Advisors to oversee PMI in Malawi, one representing CDC and one representing USAID. In addition, two Foreign Service Nationals (FSNs) work as part of the PMI team as Program Management Specialists in support of the management and administration of PMI activities. All PMI staff members are part of a single inter-agency team led by the USAID Mission Director or his designee in country. The PMI team shares responsibility for development and implementation of PMI strategies and work plans, coordination with national authorities, managing collaborating agencies and supervising day-to-day activities. Candidates for Resident Advisor positions (whether initial hires or replacements) will be evaluated and/or interviewed jointly by USAID and CDC, and both agencies will be involved in hiring decisions, with the final decision made by the individual agency.

The PMI professional staff works together to oversee all technical and administrative aspects of PMI, including finalizing details of the project design, implementing malaria prevention and treatment activities, monitoring and evaluation of outcomes and impact, and reporting of results and providing guidance to PMI partners.

The PMI lead in-country is the USAID Mission Director. The two PMI Advisors, one from USAID and one from CDC, report to the Senior USAID Health Officer for day-to-day leadership, and work together as a part of a single interagency team. The technical expertise housed in Atlanta and Washington guides PMI programmatic efforts and thus overall technical guidance for both Resident Advisors falls to the PMI staff in Atlanta and Washington. Since CDC resident advisors are CDC employees (CDC USDD – 38), responsibility for completing official performance reviews lies with the CDC Country Director who is expected to rely upon input from PMI staff across the two agencies that work closely day in day out with the CDC Resident Advisor and thus best positioned to comment on the Resident Advisor's performance.

The two PMI resident advisors are both based within the USAID health office and are expected to spend approximately half their time sitting with and providing technical support to the national malaria programs and partners.

Locally-hired staff to support PMI activities either in Ministries or in USAID will be approved by the USAID Mission Director. Because of the need to adhere to specific country policies and USAID accounting regulations, any transfer of PMI funds directly to Ministries or host governments will need to be approved by the USAID Mission Director and Controller in addition to the PMI Controller.

In early 2012, the PMI Malawi team experienced substantial staff turnover as both Resident Advisors and a couple members of headquarters support staff at USAID and CDC departed the PMI Malawi team. The CDC Resident Advisor's position was filled in January and USAID Resident Advisor's in April 2013. The position of Program Management Specialist was filled in June 2013 after being vacant for four months.

Planned activities with FY 2014 funding and justification ($1,906,000)

- Support to CDC for staffing ($550,000);
- Support to USAID for staffing ($800,000);
- Support to USAID for administration and technical oversight ($460,000);
- Support to CDC for eight temporary duty assignments (TDY), including four TDYs to oversee operational research, two for entomological monitoring, one for developing scope of work for vector control strategy, and one for M&E to monitor improvements in malaria surveillance and integration of malaria laboratory data in the electronic records system ($96,000).

Table 1

President's Malaria Initiative - Malawi
Budget Breakdown by Partner - FY 2014

Partner	Geographical Area	Activity	Budget ($)	%
DELIVER	Nationwide	Procure LLINs, SP, ACTs, RDTs, parenteral artesunate, ancillary supplies, and ANC supplies; support end-use verification surveys and Global Fund-PMI supply chain.	$9,762,000	51%
PSI	Nationwide	Support LLIN distribution including assistance for mass distribution and post-campaign survey.	$1,006,000	5%
AIRS	Nationwide	Provide technical assistance to the NMCP to implement integrated vector management strategy.	$75,000	0%
MalariaCare	Nationwide	Support outreach training and supportive supervision for microscopy and RDTs.	$1,000,000	5%
SSDI Communications	Nationwide	Support national-level BCC on diagnosis and treatment, LLIN ownership and use, and IPTp uptake.	$700,000	4%
SSDI Services	Nationwide	Support strengthening of focused antenatal care programs, and a community-based campaign to increase uptake of malaria prevention and control interventions.	$1,900,000	10%
SSDI Systems	Nationwide	Assist TWG operations via logistical and operational support, support NMCP to attend short courses and participate in regional and international meetings, support leadership and governance strengthening of NMCP, strengthen M&E, and support the National Health Accounts study with focus on malaria subaccounts.	$530,000	3%
Local Mission APS	Selected districts	Support community-based organizations to engage with school-aged children in malaria prevention activities.	$200,000	1%
TBD	Nationwide	Support for anticipated IPTp policy update in 2015.	$100,000	1%
Peace Corps	Nationwide	Support for malaria prevention and control activities.	$30,000	0%

TRAction Project	Nationwide	Support for PBI impact evaluation.	$250,000	1%
World Bank	Nationwide	Support to strengthen GoM financial management systems.	$250,000	1%
Malawi Local Capacity Development	Nationwide	Support for pre-service training of new pharmacy technicians.	$250,000	1%
TBD	Nationwide	Support for the Demographic and Health Survey.	$459,000	2%
CDC/MAC	Nationwide	Support for operations research on IPTp, entomological monitoring, and CDC staffing	$1,346,000	7%
USAID	Nationwide	Support for USAID staffing and program costs.	$1,260,000	7%
Total			**$19,118,000**	**100%**

Table 2
President's Malaria Initiative - Malawi
Planned Obligations for FY 2014

Proposed Activity	Mechanism	Budget		Geographical area	Description
		Total $	Commodity $		
PREVENTIVE ACTIVITIES					
Insecticide-Treated Nets					
Procurement of ITNs for routine distribution	DELIVER	$2,872,000	$2,872,000	Nationwide	Procure 800,000 ITNs for continuous distribution through routine channels
Distribution of ITNs for routine systems	PSI	$856,000		Nationwide	Distribute 800,000 ITNs to clinics for routine distribution systems
Technical assistance for 2015 planned mass campaign	PSI	$150,000		Nationwide	Support NMCP to plan for 2015 ITN mass distribution campaign, including a consultant on micro-planning; supportive supervision during the campaign and monitoring of the process
SUBTOTAL ITNs		**$3,878,000**	**$2,872,000**		
Indoor Residual Spraying					
Technical assistance for IRS activities	AIRS	$75,000		Nationwide	Technical assistance to the NMCP to implement evidence-based integrated vector management strategy
SUBTOTAL IRS		**$75,000**			
Malaria in Pregnancy					
Procurement of SP	DELIVER	$290,000	$290,000	Nationwide	Procure and distribute approximately 2.4 million doses of quality-assured SP for malaria prevention in pregnancy
Procurement of directly observed therapy (DOT) supplies	SSDI-Services	$50,000	$50,000	Nationwide	Procure ANC supplies (cups and water buckets) to improve IPTp uptake
Strengthening IPTp through support for focused antenatal care	SSDI-Services	$300,000		Nationwide	Support for the strengthening of the national focused antenatal care programs and proper implementation of the new IPTp guidelines; including quarterly supervision

Support to anticipated IPTp policy change	TBD	$100,000		Nationwide	Support to IPTp policy change in line with anticipated WHO recommendations on new medicines, including developing and printing of new policy guidelines and job aids, according to new evidence base
SUBTOTAL MIP		**$740,000**	**$340,000**		
SUBTOTAL PREVENTIVE		**$4,693,000**	**$3,212,000**		
Case Management					
Diagnosis					
Strengthen microscopy and RDTs as part of larger laboratory strengthening effort	MalariaCare	$1,000,000		Nationwide	Support outreach training and support supervision for microscopy and RDTs as part of larger laboratory strengthening efforts, including training and supervision of HSAs on RDTs in non-SSDI districts
Procurement of RDTs	DELIVER	$2,050,000	$2,050,000	Nationwide	Procure and distribute 3.3 million RDTs for health facilities and village health clinics using the Global Fund-PMI supply chain
Procurement of ancillary diagnostic supplies	DELIVER	$150,000		Nationwide	Procure and distribute ancillary diagnostic supplies through Global Fund-PMI supply chain
SUBTOTAL - Diagnosis		**$3,200,000**	**$2,050,000**		
Treatment					
Procurement of ACTs	DELIVER	$2,500,000	$2,500,000	Nationwide	Procure and distribute approximately 2 million doses of ACTs for health facilities and village health clinics through PMI-supported supply chain
Strengthen facility and community-based services	SSDI-Services	$450,000		Nationwide	Technical assistance for improving the case management systems at facility and community level using quality improvement procedures
SUBTOTAL - Treatment		**$2,950,000**	**$2,500,000**		
Pharmaceutical Management					
PMI-Global Fund supply chain	DELIVER	$1,100,000		Nationwide	Support management, oversight, and distribution of PMI-procured case management commodities

Technical assistance to strengthen national supply chain	DELIVER	$700,000		Nationwide	Support technical assistance for strengthening the national supply chain
SUBTOTAL - Pharmaceutical Management		**$1,800,000**			
SUBTOTAL CASE MANAGEMENT		**$7,950,000**	**$4,550,000**		
HIV & Malaria					
SUBTOTAL HIV and Malaria					
Monitoring and Evaluation					
Demographic and Health Survey	TBD	$459,000		Nationwide	Support for the 2015 Demographic and Health Survey
Strengthen routine HMIS for malaria data	SSDI-Services	$200,000		Nationwide	Continue to strengthen routine HMIS for malaria data collection
End-Use Verification Surveys	DELIVER	$100,000		Nationwide	Support for quarterly monitoring of PMI-procured commodities at health facility level
Entomological monitoring	CDC	$350,000		Seven IRS districts	Continue support to entomologic monitoring in up to seven districts where NMCP is spraying
SUBTOTAL - M&E		**$1,109,000**			
Operational Research					
Monitoring molecular markers	CDC	$75,000		Selected districts	Support monitoring *Plasmodium falciparum* resistance markers for pregnant women at ANC
Delivery cross-sectional survey monitoring effectiveness of IPTp	CDC	$275,000		Three selected districts	Support delivery cross-sectional survey to monitor effectiveness of IPTp with SP in areas with high SP resistance
SUBTOTAL - OR		**$350,000**			
SUBTOTAL - M&E and OR		**$1,459,000**			
Behavior Change Communication					

Nationwide BCC Activities	SSDI-Communications	$700,000		Nationwide	Support for national-level BCC on diagnosis and treatment; ITN ownership and use; and IPTp uptake
Community-based BCC activities for ITN use	SSDI-Services	$500,000		15 SSDI Districts	Provide small grants to NGOs to promote ITN use and net care and repair among all household members
Community-based BCC activities for IPTp	SSDI-Services	$100,000		15 SSDI Districts	Provide small grants to NGOs to promote uptake of IPTp and improve ANC attendance by late or non-attending pregnant women
Malaria prevention activities targeted to adolescents	Local Mission APS	$200,000		Machinga District	Provide small grants to CBOs to engage school-aged children in malaria prevention activities
Continue with community level pre-referral BCC	SSDI-Services	$200,000		15 SSDI Districts	Support community level BCC on initiation and completion of pre-referral treatment for severe malaria
SUBTOTAL BCC		**$1,700,000**			

Health Systems Strengthening and NMCP Capacity building

Logistical and operational support to NMCP secretariat	SSDI-Systems	$100,000		Nationwide	Support to NMCP to hold technical working group and research dissemination meetings and support basic operational functioning.
Build leadership and management capapcity	SSDI-Systems	$30,000		Nationwide	Support activities to build leadership and management skills in the NMCP.
Support NMCP for courses and meetings	SSDI-Systems	$30,000		Nationwide	Support NMCP to participate in short courses and regional and international meetings to expand knowledge base
M&E strengthening actvities	SSDI-Systems	$160,000		Nationwide	Support M&E strengthening activities to support implementation of the DHIS.
National Health Accounts	SSDI-Systems	$110,000		Nationwide	Support to National Health Accounts study focusing on the malaria subaccounts.
Infrastructure improvements of selected health facilities, focus on ANC and labor and delivery settings	SSDI-Services	$100,000		15 SSDI districts	Support small-scale infrastructure improvements of selected health facilities, focus on ANC and labor and delivery settings to improve patient experience, address referral deficiencies, enhance health outcomes, decrease loss to follow-up.
Support development of electronic data systems	SSDI-Systems	$100,000		15 SSDI districts	Support expansion of existing electronic data systems in Malawi to allow better tracking of confirmed malaria cases, guide quantification and forecasting, and implement the DHIS 2 system.

Contribute to Impact Evaluation of Performance Based Incentives pilot	Translating Research into Action (TRAction) Project	$250,000		Three districts	Contribute to impact evaluation of performance-based incentives pilot in three pilot districts.
Public Financial Management reforms	World Bank	$250,000		Nationwide	Contribute to Public Financial Management reforms to strengthen budgeting, expenditure tracking and reporting on key health programs, including malaria.
Peace Corps volunteers	Peace Corps	$30,000		Nationwide	Support two Peace Corps volunteers to work with the NMCP plus funding for small project activities.
Support pre-service training of pharmacy technicians	Malawi Local Capacity Development	$250,000		Nationwide	Support pre-service training of 24 new pharmacy technicians. Pharmacy technicians will be trained in logistics management, drug storage, drug dispensing, inventory, reporting, etc.
SUBTOTAL - HSS and Capacity Bldg		**$1,410,000**			
In-country Staffing and Administration					
CDC staffing	CDC	$550,000			Support CDC staffing
USAID staffing	USAID	$800,000			Support USAID staffing
Admin & Oversight	USAID	$460,000			Support USAID program costs
CDC TDY	CDC	$96,000			Support eight temporary duty assignments including the annual MOP meeting and provide technical assistance for entomology activities and operational research
SUBTOTAL - In-Country Staffing		**$1,906,000**			
GRAND TOTAL		**$19,118,000**	**$7,762,000**		